UNIQUE California

A Guide to the State's Quirks, Charisma, and Character

Richard Harris

John Muir Publications
Santa Fe, New Mexico

John Muir Publications, P.O. Box 613, Santa Fe, NM 87504

Printed in the United States of America

First edition. First printing September 1994

Library of Congress Cataloging-in-Publication Data

Harris, Richard, 1947–
Unique California : a guide to the state's quirks, charisma, and
character / Richard Harris. — 1st ed.
p. cm.
Includes index.
ISBN 1-56261-179-8 : $10.95
1. California—Guidebooks. I. Title.
F859.3.H35 1994
917.9404'53—dc20 94-20048
CIP

Production: Ellen Olmsted, Chris Brigman
Editorial: Elizabeth Wolf, Nancy Gillan
Design: Ken Wilson
Typography: Marcie Pottern
Illustrations: Chris Brigman
Photo Research: Deborah Dunn
Typefaces: Stone Serif, Oz Handicraft
Printer: Quebecor/Semline

Distributed to the book trade by
W. W. Norton & Co.
New York, New York

Front cover photo: Leo de Wys Inc./James Hackett
Front cover photo inset: Leo de Wys Inc./E.C. Stangler
Back cover photo: Bob Yarbrough/San Diego Convention &
Visitors Bureau

CONTENTS

INTRODUCTION

California has it all. The most populous state in the United States, California boasts the second-largest city and no fewer than 13 of the 25 fastest-growing cities according to the 1990 U.S. Census. Elsewhere in the state, the Mojave Desert presents arid and alien landscapes so devoid of population that the Navy tests experimental weapons there. Side-by-side with the polyglot sophistication of the Bay Area and the palm-lined shopping-mall civilization of the Southland, you'll find wild areas unsurpassed in their natural beauty—legendary beaches secluded on remote, rocky headlands; forests of majestic redwood trees, the largest living things on earth; the highest mountain peak between Anchorage and Mexico City.

Visitors to Southern California realize immediately that they're not in Kansas anymore when, driving into the city from the surrounding desert, they are confronted by the fact that metropolitan Los Angeles has more automobiles—upwards of 9 million—than any other city on earth. And they all seem to be heading for the same place. Southlanders spend a lot of time in their cars. Appropriately enough in the city that provides most of the world's cinematic car chases and shoot-outs, a sense of make-believe sets in as the windshield starts seeming like a movie screen.

And then there's Northern California, a completely different land where ecotourism comes easy. You'll find groves of the world's oldest trees, rocky points overlooking spectacular ocean views, and the dramatic bare-rock crags of the Sierra Nevada Mountains, all within easy driving distance of San Francisco, California's second city—smaller, older, and in many ways more sophisticated than L.A. In these pages you will also discover the state's less touristy side, the great Central Valley, which ranks as the number-one ranching and farming area in the United States.

San Francisco Convention & Visitors Bureau

Coit Tower dominates San Francisco's North Beach skyline

Unique California is a compilation of one-of-a-kind destinations, historical insights, and fun facts from the lunatic fringe of the American frontier. It's designed for curious and adventuresome travelers of all ages. Open to any page and you will find readable, entertaining information. The index guides you to specific topics and sites. The table of contents is organized so you can tell at a glance what subjects are covered in each section. However you choose to use this book, you'll soon discover what is unique about California.

Roy Murphy/USDA Forest Service

The towering redwood is California's state tree

CALIFORNIA

Population:
29,760,021

Area:
158,706 sq. miles

Capital:
Sacramento

Nickname:
Golden State

Date of Statehood:
September 9, 1850

Highest Elevation:
Mt. Whitney, 14,494 ft.

State Flower:
Golden poppy

State Bird:
California valley quail

State Tree:
California redwood

State Motto:
Eureka
(I Have Found It)

THEN AND NOW

100 Million Years Ago–A.D. 1542

Moving Mountains

Castle Crags rise out of the Cascade Mountains

Shasta Cascade Wonderland Assoc.

High in the arid San Bernardino Mountains near Palm Springs, hikers can find rocks embedded with sea shells—more than 80 miles from the sea. They prove that California rose out of the Pacific Ocean within the last 100 million years. Although that may sound like a long time, the age of dinosaurs was nearly over before upheavals began lifting the Sierra Nevada mountains and central valley above sea level.

Two of the tectonic plates that form the earth's surface—the North American Plate and the Pacific Plate—began moving very slowly, the plate that forms the floor of the Pacific Ocean sliding under North America's land mass. Earthquake faults fractured, rumbled, and little by little lifted the Coast Range out of the sea to build the California coast as we know it. The process continues today. While some people worry about the possibility of earthquakes destroying California, it's good to remember that today's seismic activity is part of the same series of terrain-altering events that created the land in the first place. Easy come, easy go.

In the Miocene period—25 million to 11 million years ago—northern Sierra Nevada volcanos built that great mountain range to its present height, and lava flows created much of the land that is now Northern California. The volcanos also deposited the gold ore that would shape California history millions of years later.

The wall of mountains stopped the ocean's moisture from reaching inland. Rain stopped falling on the land east of the mountains about 16 million years ago, and the Mojave Desert was created. Rain that did not reach the desert fell along the newly created coastline, which became lush rain forest. Over millions of years, decaying vegetation from this primeval jungle formed underground pools of liquid carbon deposits, which make up the rich oil deposits that lie under Southern California today.

A Sticky Situation

Tar from the subterranean oil fields has bubbled to the surface for the last 40,000 years. In fact, the gooey ooze has been part of the California landscape for so long that new species have evolved around it. Consider the California petroleum fly, whose larvae live in pools of crude oil that would kill most other life forms, feeding on other insects trapped in the oil.

Over the millennia, a lot more than just insects have been snared in oil seeps, especially at the famous **La Brea Tar Pits**. Rain collects on the surface of the tar, disguising it as a freshwater pond. Prehistoric animals who wandered too far into the "water" have been preserved for tens of thousands of years in the tar. Life-size sculptures of a giant sloth and a mastodon in their death throes have been placed at the tar pits—now virtually the only natural landscape for miles—to help passersby visualize the dramas that took place there long ago. Skeletons dredged from the muck (and other exhibits) are displayed in the **George Page Museum of La Brea Discoveries** beside the tar pits.

Humans used asphalt from the tar pits long before anybody was interested in refining oil into gasoline. Indians used it to waterproof their woven baskets. The original Spanish grant deeding the area around La Brea Tar Pits to a wealthy rancher in the 18th century reserved the right of every Los Angeles resident to use the tar for repairing sails and roofs. ***FYI:*** 5801 Wilshire Boulevard; 213-936-2230.

Los Angeles CVB/Michele & Tom Grimm

Over the centuries, many creatures have been trapped in the sticky ooze of La Brea Tar Pits

1542–1821: The Spanish Colonial Era

1542: The viceroy of New Spain (Mexico) sent two ships, the *San Salvador* and the *Victoria*, under the command of Portuguese-born sea captain Juan Rodriguez Cabrillo, to explore North America's west coast in search of a "Northwest Passage" between the Atlantic and Pacific Oceans. Cabrillo and his crew landed at the site of present-day San Diego on September 28, 1542, the first Europeans to set foot on California soil. They continued up the coast to visit the area where Santa Monica is located today, as well as Catalina Island and the Channel Islands. Cabrillo died on January 3 of the following year, from injuries sustained in a fall, and was buried on San Miguel Island. The expedition's pilot, Bartolomé Ferrelo, continued sailing north and mapped the entire coast of California before returning to New Spain four months later.

Cabrillo called the land Alta (Upper) California. Both Alta and Baja (Lower) California were named after a mythical land that was the setting for a popular Spanish epic poem. Although Spain laid claim to the territory of California with the Cabrillo expedition, no Spanish colonists would settle there for more than two centuries.

1579: Sir Francis Drake claimed California for England after anchoring in the bay that is now named after him on the coast of present-day Marin County. He spent 36 days there repairing his storm-damaged ship, the *Golden Hind*. During that time, he established friendly relations with the local Indians and named the land New Albion. The British never established a colony there, either, and Drake's claim was ignored.

San Diego Convention & Visitors Bureau

Mission San Diego de Alcala was the first of California's 21 missions

1769: Fearing that the Pacific coast would be claimed by the Russians, the government of New Spain sent a "Sacred Expedition" into the mostly unexplored California wilderness to establish mission churches. The expedition leader, Gaspar de Portolá, commanded 300 soldiers and traveled with a herd of horses, mules, and cattle. The troop's spiritual leader was Junipero

Serra, a 56-year-old Franciscan friar and former philosophy professor. They crossed 1,500 miles of arid mountains and desert to rendezvous with supply ships, and founded San Diego, the first European settlement in California. The Sacred Expedition went on to found a second settlement at Monterey. Father Serra built a mission at San Diego and remained in the new land to build eight other missions over the next 15 years along the the Camino Real (Royal Road) up the California coast. (See page 34 for more on the missions.)

1776: As the American Revolution broke out 3,000 miles away, an expedition of 240 Spanish soldiers and settlers led by Captain Juan Bautiste de Anza and Father Francisco Garcés set out from a mission near the site of present-day Tucson and traveled north to found the settlement that would become San Francisco.

1781: Forty-four colonists from the Mexican state of Sinaloa, mostly of Native American and African American descent, banded together to establish El Pueblo de Nuestra Señora la Reina de Los Angeles (the Town of Our Lady the Queen of the Angels), which would become Los Angeles.

1821: Mexico won independence from Spain. Life in distant California remained unchanged, but Spanish colonists there officially declared their loyalty to Mexico the following year.

1826–1900: The Mexican War, the Gold Rush, and Statehood

1826: Mountain Man Jedediah Smith's beaver-trapping expedition entered the San Joaquin Valley—the first explorers from the United States to set foot in California. They were arrested as spies and later banished from the state.

California had a total of 3,270 non-Indian residents.

1841: Wagon trains such as the Bidwell-Bartleson and Workman-Rowland companies began carrying pioneers from the United States to California. The non-Indian population of California grew from 6,000 to 7,000 in the next five years.

1846: Twenty-four settlers from the United States seized Sonoma in a series of raids known as the Bear Flag Revolt and declared California an independent republic. The new republic lasted only 30 days before word arrived that the United States was at war with Mexico. As U.S. battleships seized Monterey, then San Francisco and Los Angeles, the Bear Flag revolutionaries left to join the U.S. Army. The revolutionary banner, on which a golden grizzly bear and a star were painted in blackberry juice, would later be adopted as the California state flag.

Wagon trains kept coming to California. The Donner party, stranded by snowstorms while attempting to cross the Sierra Nevada, remained trapped in the frozen mountains from early November of 1846 until April 1847. Of 87 pioneers who started out with the wagon train, 47 survived—some by eating the flesh of their companions who had frozen to death.

1848: On January 13, a month before Mexico ceded California to the United States as part of the treaty that ended the Mexican War, the Mexican authorities in California surrendered to Major John C. Fremont, who would become the territorial governor and later a U.S. senator. In a crowning moment of historical irony, James Marshall found a nugget at Sutter's sawmill on January 24—less than two weeks after the surrender. Over three centuries, the Spanish conquistadors and colonists had found no trace of gold.

The Bettmann Archive

By the late 1800s, San Francisco's population was nearly 300,000

Marshall and his partner, John Sutter, neither kept their discovery secret nor staked a claim. When the news got out, more than 80,000 adventurers stampeded west from the United States to seek their fortune in the gold fields. Squatters and prospectors took over the land where Marshall and Sutter had operated their sawmill. Within five years, the gold fields yielded more than $200 million worth of ore; but Sutter's Mill went bankrupt, and the owners died broke.

1850: Admitted to the Union on September 9 as the 31st state, California was declared to be a Free State (without slavery) under a federal law known as the Clay Compromise. The population of California reached 92,000. San Francisco had 24,000 residents; Los Angeles, 1,600.

1860: California's population reached 380,000. San Francisco had 57,000 residents; Los Angeles, 4,000.

1869: Completion of the first transcontinental railroad linked California to the rest of the United States. The railroad brought prosperity to central California farmers by providing a way to ship produce to eastern markets. The Pacific Standard Time zone was established to make railroad timetables possible. (Before that, people simply reckoned the time of day according to when the sun reached its zenith, so the time was a bit different in each town.)

1870: California's population reached 560,000. San Francisco had 149,000 residents; Los Angeles, 5,700.

1880: The population of California climbed to 865,000. San Francisco had 234,000 residents; Los Angeles, 11,000.

1890: California's population was 1,213,000. San Francisco had 299,000 residents; Los Angeles, 50,000.

1900: The population of California was 1,485,000. San Francisco had 343,000 residents, and Los Angeles, 102,000. Overall, in the fifty years since statehood, California's population had grown by 1,600 percent—and the boom was just beginning!

1900–1945

The great earthquake and fire of 1906 nearly leveled San Francisco

1906: An earthquake estimated at 8.3 on the Richter scale—the most powerful quake ever to hit a U.S. city—rocked San Francisco in the early morning hours of April 18. Several of the city's tallest buildings collapsed, but the greatest destruction was yet to come. Crumbled fireplaces, burst furnaces, and ruptured gas mains started fires that raged through San Francisco for three days, destroying an area of 490 city blocks. Five hundred people lost their lives.

Meanwhile, in Southern California, filmmakers George Van Guysling and Otis M. Gove started California's first film studio at a ranch on the outskirts of Los Angeles (population 102,000). The ranch land would later become the city of Hollywood.

1915: The first transcontinental telephone call was made from San Francisco to New York.

1916: Aircraft engineers Glenn Martin, Donald Douglas, Allan Loughead, and John K. Northrop won small government contracts to build biplanes for the U.S. Army. They built their factories in southern California because the cost of living was low and labor was cheap. Their companies became Martin-Marietta, Douglas, and Lockheed—the largest aerospace companies in the world.

1918: The Save the Redwoods League, one of California's first environmental groups, was founded. The league's efforts would later result in the creation of more than 135,000 acres of state parks.

1921: Oil was discovered on a ranch at Signal Hill, near present-day Long Beach. The largest oil field ever found in California, it was soon producing 250,000 barrels of oil per day. Oil quickly became California's largest industry. The population of the Los Angeles area surpassed that of the San Francisco area for the first time.

1928: Herbert Hoover became the first Californian to be elected president of the United States. His Republican administration became embroiled in a scandal of monumental proportions, setting a precedent that all later presidents from California have followed.

1930: As drought turned Oklahoma and other midwestern states into a "Dust Bowl," people there were driven from their farms. Thousands headed west to seek work in the rich farmlands of California's Central Valley, only to find desperately poor living conditions and exploitation by wealthy landowners.

Bancroft Library, UC-Berkeley

Shipyard workers in the 1940s were part of the defense industry boom in California

1941: After Japanese planes bombed Pearl Harbor, drawing the United States into World War II, hysterical Washington politicians feared that Japanese Americans might become saboteurs or spies. Under a new law, 93,000 California residents of Japanese ancestry (including American-born U.S. citizens) were taken to "War Relocation Camps" in remote areas of the Southwest and other parts of the United States and imprisoned there for three years. San Diego and San Francisco served as headquarters for American forces in the Pacific throughout the war.

1943: The Zoot Suit Riots, a series of violent clashes between young Mexican American residents and U.S. soldiers and sailors from bases in the area, ripped through Los Angeles for 11 days. No one died, but animosities arising from the event live on half a century later in the Hispanic *barrios* of East L.A.

UPI/Bettmann

Los Angelenos of Japanese descent prepare to be relocated to Manzanar internment camp during World War II

1945: Representatives from fifty nations met at the San Francisco Opera House for two months of discussions on how to ensure world peace. On June 26, 1945, they signed the charter creating the United Nations.

1946–1962: The Postwar Era

1946: The population of Southern California skyrocketed as returning World War II veterans chose to start new lives in the land of palm trees and year-round sunshine. Approximately 500,000 people moved to the Los Angeles metropolitan area within the next five years.

California native Richard Nixon, a young lawyer just out of the Navy, was elected to the U.S. Congress after charging that his opponent, Helen Gahagan Douglas, was "soft on Communism."

1947: Anti-Communist paranoia swept the motion picture industry as the House Un-American Activities Committee of the U.S. Congress investigated a supposedly subversive plot to infiltrate the media. Unfounded allegations ruined the careers of movie stars, directors, and producers. A group of screenwriters known as the Hollywood Ten refused to testify before the committee and were imprisoned on contempt charges.

1949: The University of California required its faculty and staff to sign a loyalty oath affirming that they were not Communists. After a lengthy controversy, 31 professors were fired for refusing to sign the oath.

1952: A federal court ruled that the University of California's loyalty oath requirement was unconstitutional. The professors who had refused to sign were reinstated to their jobs. Meanwhile, however, California lawmakers changed the state constitution to require loyalty oaths of all public employees. (The state's loyalty oath requirement would be ruled unconstitutional in 1967. David Saxon, one of the professors who had been fired for refusing to take the oath, would become president of the University of California in 1975.)

Smithsonian Institute

California Congressman Richard Nixon was elected vice president under President Eisenhower in 1952

California Congressman Richard M. Nixon was elected vice president of the United States under President Eisenhower, a position he would hold for eight years.

Los Angeles Convention & Visitors Bureau

Sleeping Beauty's Castle at Disneyland

1955: Disneyland opened. The largest amusement park in the world at the time, it attracted more than 1 million visitors in its first six months of operation and helped make Southern California one of America's top tourist destinations.

1957: In a strange counterpoint to the anti-Communist paranoia that had been sweeping the state for a decade, "beatniks" following the lead of Jack Kerouac, Henry Miller, and other counterculture heros of the time started moving to the San Francisco and Big Sur areas. San Francisco's gay community began to develop at the same time, and in an era characterized by conformity, Northern California began taking on a reputation as the alternative lifestyle capital of America.

1958: California got its first major league baseball teams as the Brooklyn Dodgers moved to Los Angeles and the New York Giants moved to San Francisco. Two years later, the Los Angeles Dodgers would win the World Series.

1960: Richard Nixon ran for president of the United States but lost to Senator John F. Kennedy.

1962: California replaced New York as the most populous state in the United States.

Richard Nixon ran for governor of California but lost to incumbent Pat Brown.

John Steinbeck, California's greatest living novelist, was awarded the Nobel Prize for literature.

Cesar Chavez, spokesperson for Chicano migrant farm workers (as Steinbeck had been for the Okie migrant workers thirty years before) formed the National Farm Workers' Union.

Recent Times

1964: The Free Speech Movement swept the campus of the University of California at Berkeley. A ban on soliciting funds for political causes triggered demonstrations, sit-ins, and the takeover of the university's administration building by more than 700 student activists, who were taken into custody in the largest mass arrest in California history. Demonstrations continued over a variety of First Amendment and students' rights issues. In the years to come, Berkeley's Free Speech Movement would form the prototype for student demonstrations throughout the United States.

1965: Police brutality during the drunk-driving arrest of a black motorist by white LAPD officers ignited long-standing racial tensions in the Watts area of Los Angeles. Six days of rioting left 34 people dead and more than 1,000 injured. Property damage exceeded $40 million.

1967: San Francisco's Haight-Ashbury district, with its big old Victorian homes perfectly suited for communal living, became the center of the hippie movement. More than 100,000 young people from all parts of the United States were drawn to the city during the much-publicized "Summer of Love" for peace, love, drugs, and free Grateful Dead concerts in Golden Gate Park.

Karen Elyse Fenton/San Francisco Convention & Visitors Bureau

The Haight-Ashbury district, sans flower children

In another strange cultural counterpoint, archconservative actor/politician Ronald Reagan was elected governor of California.

The ship *Queen Mary* docked at Long Beach, California, where it has stayed ever since.

1968: Richard Nixon made a spectacular political comeback, becoming the second Californian elected president of the United States.

1973: Tom Bradley became the first black mayor of Los Angeles.

1974: President Richard Nixon was forced to resign under threat of impeachment because of the Watergate scandal. He retired to his "western White House," in San Clemente, California.

1977: Gay-rights activist Harvey Milk was elected to San Francisco's city council, the first openly gay person to hold that office.

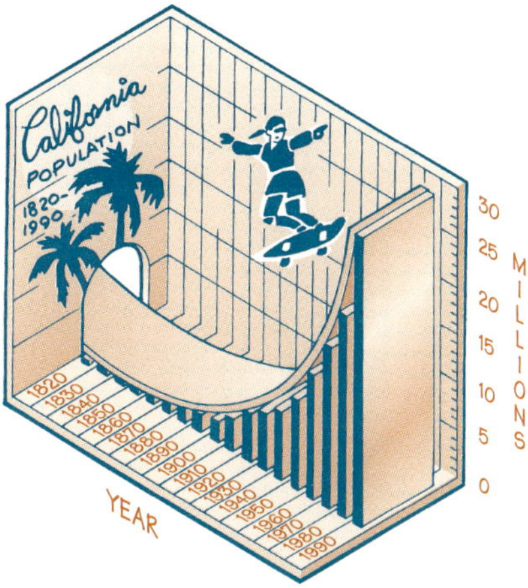

California's population has exploded over the last forty years.

1978: Harvey Milk and San Francisco Mayor George Moscone were assassinated at City Hall by conservative politician Dan White. When the court sentenced White to only five years in prison for the double murder, it sparked the "White Night Riot" in which 50,000 angry San Franciscans clashed with police and took over City Hall.

Voters passed Proposition 13, a controversial amendment to the state constitution that limited tax increases. Rapidly rising real estate prices had caused property taxes to skyrocket until many old-timers could not afford to keep their homes. Proposition 13 limited property taxes to 1975-76 levels except when the property was improved or resold. After the amendment passed, a new problem arose: local governments could not raise taxes to pay the rising costs of city and county services. Inadequate tax revenues have remained a problem for California government on all levels.

1979: Dianne Feinstein was elected mayor of San Francisco, the first woman to hold that office.

1980: Former California governor Ronald Reagan was elected president of the United States, the third Californian to hold that office.

1989: An earthquake centered just south of the San Francisco Bay area—the strongest since 1906—caused widespread damage. Motorists were crushed when city freeways collapsed.

1994: An earthquake in the Los Angeles area—the strongest in twenty years—caused shopping malls to collapse and crippled the city's freeway system. Few lives were lost because the quake struck in the early morning hours of a holiday Monday.

THE NATURAL WORLD

John Muir (1838–1914)

More places in California have been named after John Muir than any other person—saints included.

The great naturalist John Muir

National Park Service

The Scottish-born father of California's environmental movement arrived in San Francisco in 1868. His roundabout journey had taken nearly three years. A young freelance writer in Indiana, he walked 1,000 miles gathering material on the post-Civil War South. He reached Florida after seven weeks, only to fall ill with malaria. Observations of bird and plant life during his convalescence on a Gulf Coast island sparked his lifelong passion for nature. He sailed to Central America and then up the Pacific coast to California, where he made his home for the next 46 years.

John Muir dedicated his life to exploring the Sierra Nevada and wrote numerous books about his wilderness experiences, including *The Mountains of California* (1894), *My First Summer in the Sierra* (1911), and *The Yosemite* (1912). Single-handedly, he campaigned to have Yosemite declared a national park and persuaded Presidents Grover Cleveland and Theodore Roosevelt to create a series of federal forest reservations, the forerunners of today's national forest system. The Sierra Club, which grew from Muir's conservation lobbying efforts, has become one of the world's largest environmental action groups.

Robert Szaro/USDA Forest Service

It's not Malibu: Muir Beach in Marin County

One wild area where Muir's spirit lives on is **Muir Woods**, a 550-acre park in Marin County containing one of the most impressive redwood groves anywhere; the woods meet the ocean at driftwood-strewn **Muir Beach**.

Other namesake spots include the **John Muir Trail** (which runs the length of the Sierra Nevada), Sequoia National Park's **Muir Grove**, Kings Canyon National Park's **Muir Pass**, and Yosemite National Park's **Muir Gorge**.

Muir's home, preserved as it was at the time of his death, shows visitors where the naturalist lived in Victorian comfort between solitary high-mountain forays. The house, now part of **John Muir National Historic Site**, is at 4202 Alhambra Avenue in the town of Martinez.

Redwoods

California's redwoods, the tallest trees on earth, have reached heights of 367 feet. There are two subspecies of the giant trees, both found only in California. *Sequoia sempervirens* grows in the coastal mountains along a 200-mile stretch of Route 101 from the town of Leggett to the Oregon state line, including Humboldt State Park and Redwood National Park. The trees have a life span of up to 2,200 years—some have lived since the time of the Roman Empire and the dawn of the Christian era. *Sequoia gigantea* grows farther south and inland, in the high mountains of the Sierra Nevada. The best places to see them are in Yosemite, Kings Canyon, and Sequoia National Parks. They live a thousand years longer than the coastal redwoods; some sequoias living today were seedlings when King David ruled Jerusalem in Old Testament times.

Loggers have been cutting redwoods for lumber since the Spanish mission period. Foreseeing the danger of extinction for the great trees, Sierra Club founder John Muir and a coalition known as the Save the Redwoods League campaigned for the preservation of large redwood stands; their efforts were rewarded by the creation of more than 135,000 acres of state parks and 1,250,000 acres of national parks. The early conservationists' fears appear to have been justified: the road to extinction seems to be paved with gold. Big forest-products corporations, using modern logging technology, increased redwood logging on private land to unprecedented levels in the 1980s and 1990s. About 670 million board feet of redwood trees, valued at $140 million, are cut down each year.

The Bettmann Archive

California loggers hauling logs to the sawmill, 1922

Water

Richard Frear/National Park Service

The parched earth of Death Valley

Bringing Water to the Desert

Rain—or the lack thereof—makes California a land of contrasts. Parts of the northern California coast receive 100 inches of rain a year. Yet 100 miles west of San Diego, towns like El Centro and Mexicali typically go for five years between rainfalls. In fact, most of California is a desert in disguise. Even more than air quality issues or energy resources, the future of California depends on how today's legislators decide to settle competing claims on the state's limited water supply.

Development and population growth in California depend on finding new sources of water. Large-scale agriculture depends on the Central Valley Project, a network of more than 1,300 reservoirs linked by pipelines, aqueducts, and canals—the world's largest irrigation system. The All-American and Coachella Canals and the Colorado River Aqueduct all divert water from the Colorado River so efficiently that the Southwest's largest river no longer reaches its former delta on the Gulf of California. Just before it reaches the Mexican border, the last of the river is siphoned away to farms in the Imperial Valley.

The multibillion-dollar State Water Project, completed in the 1960s, created the California Aqueduct, which carries water from the mountains of Northern California to the cities and farmlands of arid Southern California. The aqueduct became a source of public outrage in 1991, when the worst drought in the state's history struck. Reservoirs serving the Bay Area ran low, forcing strict water-rationing in San Francisco in order to keep water flowing to the farmlands. Since then, reforming water allocations in the Central Valley Project has become one of the most controversial political hot potatoes in California.

Farms versus Cities

In a normal year, agriculture uses 80 percent of all the available water, leaving the cities to fight over the rest. Farmers point out that agriculture is the state's biggest industry, so it deserves top priority for water. Growing one day's supply of food for one adult takes about 1,700 gallons of water. Urban dwellers, however, contend that their water supply is more important since they make up 93 percent of the state's population, while residents of farming areas make up only 7 percent. Considering that lakes and underground aquifers are also being polluted by pesticides and fertilizers, the prospect that California will be forced to cut back on agriculture is becoming more and more likely.

California Section, California State Library Arizona Office of Tourism

Farm workers harvesting spinach

Wealthy cities such as Santa Barbara have been forced to resort to using sewage water to keep their often lavish lawns and landscaping alive. Plans have been proposed to build purification plants that would recycle sewage into fresh water for washing and drinking, as well as to pipe waste water from the Bay Area to Southern California.

What Water Shortage?

In the midst of all this fighting over water, the burgeoning desert city of Palm Springs pours phenomenal quantities of water into swimming pools, golf courses, artificial lakes and waterfalls, and devices called "misters," like air conditioners that cool and humidify outdoor air with a fine, constant spray. The water is pumped from a huge aquifer under the desert's surface. Even in the worst droughts, when San Francisco and Los Angeles water supplies dry up, Palm Springs experiences no water shortage. Because of a process called compaction, however, the aquifer beneath Palm Springs is slowly vanishing.

Palm Springs Tourism

There's never a shortage of swimming pools in Palm Springs

Life Zones

USDA/National Forest Service

Santa Lucia Mountains

Elevations

The California landscape varies in elevation from the lowest point in the lower 48 United States, a normally dry place called Badwater (282 feet *below* sea level), to the highest, Mount Whitney (14,495 feet above sea level) in Sequoia National Park. Every 1,000-foot elevation change makes a little more than 4 degrees difference in the air temperature, so when it's a sweltering 100° F in Death Valley, the temperature barely reaches above freezing on Mount Whitney's summit—even though the highest and lowest points are only 60 miles apart. The highest temperature ever recorded in California was 134°F at Death Valley in 1913, and the lowest was -45°F near Lake Tahoe in 1937.

Flora

Snow generally falls only above the 2,000-foot elevation. Hillsides covered with live oak trees are below the snow line. Ponderosa pine forests grow where snow falls but melts off between storms. Douglas fir trees grow in the high mountains, where the snow enshrouds them all winter long.

In arid areas, the occasional river or creek that spills down from the mountains creates its own ecosystem, known as a riparian habitat, with thick stands of cottonwoods and other broadleaf trees along the stream banks. Such areas, often found in hidden canyons at the foot of desert mountains, support an amazing abundance of animal and bird life.

Palm Springs Tourism

Palms line the streets of Palm Springs

The California palm, the only species of palm tree that is native to the state, grows naturally in desert oases such as Palm

Springs and Twenty-nine Palms. It grows up to 75 feet tall, and its fronds were used by desert-dwelling Indians to make thatch-roofed shelters from the sun. Hundreds of other varieties of palm trees have been imported to Southern California for landscaping.

Fauna

Many of the state's most intriguing animals live in protected desert areas such as Death Valley National Monument, Joshua Tree National Monument, and Anza-Borrego Desert State Park. The most common type of rattlesnake, the sidewinder, is small but common, so walk noisily when in the desert and never put your hands or feet where you can't see them. More benign desert dwellers include horned toads, tortoises, kangaroo rats, jackrabbits, desert bighorn sheep, pronghorn antelope, and coyotes.

The coastal forests of Northern California are home to deer, black bears, bobcats, weasels, and small, nocturnal cousins of the raccoon known as California ringtail cats—as well as coyotes. In remote reaches of the high Sierra roam elk, mountain lions, and wolverines. And coyotes.

In fact, coyotes are so adaptable that their population throughout California has reached new highs in the 1990s, even though a law more than a century old encourages ranchers to shoot them on sight at any time of year. Coyotes have learned to be city dwellers, too, successfully adapting to life in some surprisingly urban areas. They are considered the biggest animal control problem in many Southland towns, including Hollywood and Beverly Hills. Some residents have organized neighborhood save-the-coyote groups to stand up for the wild canines' right to roam city streets. According to the mythology of the Costanoan Indians who once lived in the region, human beings were created by the coyote.

Another denizen of the wilderness has not fared so well. The golden grizzly bear, depicted on the state flag, has been declared extinct in California.

Yosemite Collections, National Park Service

California's golden grizzly, now extinct

California's Coastal Environment

Tide Pools

California's most lavish display of fantastic fauna is along its 905-mile coastline. For a close look, examine the tide pools below rocky headlands at low ebb. Barnacles, limpets, and mussels cling to rocks, waiting for the sea's return; colorful starfish, octopi, crabs, and other sea-floor denizens wait in deeper pools.

Don Hoffman

Tide pools are home to many forms of sea life

Clams

Clams, California's most common beach mollusks, live under flat sand. Clams provided the main food source for coastal Indians such as the Wintuns and Costanoans, whose ancient village sites are marked by 20-foot-or-higher shell mounds. Archaeologists study these mounds, the only traces left of many tribes. Between 1916 and 1941, eight California clam species were commercially harvested on a large scale—upwards of 600,000 pounds each year. Sadly, since World War II, overharvesting, dredging, and pollution have reduced the clam population so much that neither commerical fisheries nor individual clam-lovers look for them any more.

Sea and Shore Birds

Bird life also abounds along coastal beaches and rocks. Of California's 525 bird species, more than half live along the seashore. Seagulls are the most abundant —including Heermann, Bonaparte, short-billed, ring-billed, and other gulls. The smaller California gull ranges inland from Mono Lake, west of Yosemite, to Utah's Great Salt Lake, visiting the seacoast only during winter.

Tidal flats, wetland marshes, and estuaries are home to many shore-bird species: American avocets, phalaropes, marbled godwits, sandpipers, oyster-catchers, cormorants, loons, grebes, and others.

Prince among California shore birds is the brown pelican, a once-threatened species now a common sight. Alcatraz was home to one of the west coast's largest pelican colonies before the prison was built. In Spanish, *alcatraz* means pelican.

Marine Mammals

Sea otters are native to the central California coast. These giant members of the weasel family reach 4 to 5 feet in length and are sometimes mistaken for seals. Russian and American fur-hunters killed about 5,000 a year through most of the 19th century. By 1874, sea otters were so rare that California's legislature protected them with the first endangered-species law. After a gradual comeback, sea otters today number about 1,000. Although still among California's most threatened species, they are often spotted in coastal kelp beds between Santa Barbara and Monterey.

Monterey Bay Aquarium

California's protected sea otter population is making a comeback

Seals have also returned from near-extinction along the California coast. Early 19th-century Russian hunters killed as many as 40,000 seals a year, especially California's native Guadalupe seal and the migratory Pribilof seal. Non-fur-bearing seals—including the stellar sea lion, the California sea lion, the elephant seal, and the harbor seal—were also slaughtered until, by 1833, only 54 seals were left alive on the California coast. A 1911 state law protected them and today California sea lions and harbor seals live all along the coast; a small population of huge, rare, stellar sea lions lives on remote Channel Islands National Park. Fishermen view seals as predators and oppose laws that protect their growing numbers.

Monterey Bay Aquarium

Sea otters thrive in kelp beds, like the one reproduced at the Monterey Bay Aquarium

Although gray whales are not exactly California natives, they became the official State Marine Mammal in 1976. Thousands of "pods" of three to five whales each follow the coastline on their 6,000-mile migration from the Bering Sea to Baja California. They travel within sight of land—south in December/January, north in March/April—making whale-watching a popular human pastime. Also seen along California's coast are dolphins, porpoises, humpback whales, and even blue whales, the earth's largest living creatures.

Earthquake!

Earthquake faults are cracks in the earth's crust. Huge plates of rock more than 30 miles thick, such as the one beneath most of North America, drift on the molten lava deep inside the earth, creating friction and stress along the faults. When they slip even a little bit, the jolt can cause damage over a 100-mile (or larger) radius.

Hundreds of faults underlie virtually all of California west of the Sierra Nevada. Mini-earthquakes strong enough to be felt rumble through the state at the rate of several thousand a year. Quakes intense enough to rattle objects on tables and counter tops are unusual enough to rate local news coverage. Quakes violent enough to cause death and mass destruction have struck the state six times in living memory. Most Californians accept the reality that "the Big One"—an earthquake measuring over 8.0 on the Richter scale—will strike a major California city in the near future. Some say that imminent catastrophe gives Californians a special live-for-the-moment excitement. Others simply enjoy the climate and ignore the risk.

Helpful Hint: In case you're around when the Big One separates coastal California from the mainland, you'll find complete safety instructions in the front pages of the telephone directory.

How to Measure Disasters

Seismographs, which chart movements of the ground, measure earthquake force on the Richter Scale. Each number on the scale represents ten times the magnitude, and *sixty* times the destructive energy, of the next lower digit. So San Francisco's 8.3 earthquake in 1906 was more than ten times stronger than the 7.1 quake that rocked the city in 1989. The scale was developed in 1935 by geologist Charles Richter of the California Institute of Technology. Ironically, within a few years after his death, all of Richter's books and papers were destroyed in a gas fire caused by the January 1994 Los Angeles earthquake.

California's Biggest Earthquakes

1. Owens Valley (1872)–estimated at 8.3 on the Richter scale
2. San Francisco (1906)–est. 8.3
3. Tejon Pass (1857)–est. 7.75
4. Tehachapi and Bakersfield (1952)–est. 7.7
5. Los Angeles (1994)–est. 7.2
6. San Francisco (1989)–est. 7.1
7. Hayward (1868)–est. 7.0
8. San Fernando (1971)–est. 6.6
9. Long Beach (1933)–est. 6.3
10. Santa Barbara (1925)–est. 6.3

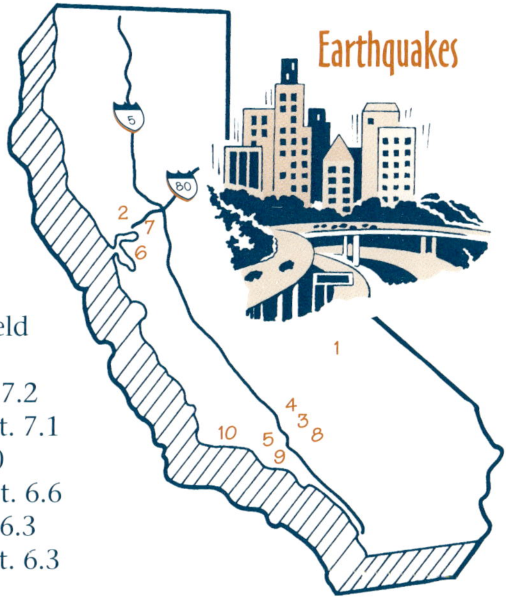

More Disasters

Besides earthquakes, California is known for its impressive array of other disasters. Dry summers and autumn's hot Santa Ana winds make Southern California's forests and brush-covered hillsides a tinderbox that often flares into wildfires, usually during September. Among the most devastating have been the 220,000-acre Matilija Canyon fire in Santa Barbara County in 1932, the deadly Griffith Park fire of 1933, the 1961 Santa Monica Mountains fire that destroyed homes in the exclusive Bel Air suburb, the twin 1970 fires that burned 325,000 acres around Los Angeles and San Diego, and the firestorms that swept Malibu and other Southland communities in 1993.

By destroying the ground cover, wildfires create the conditions for huge mudslides when the rains do come. The worst mudslide in California history destroyed the town of La Crescenta (in the San Gabriel Mountains near Los Angeles) in 1934. Mudslides frequently endanger mansions in the Bel Air hills. Flooding is also a hazard in Northern California, where the Sacramento and Russian Rivers regularly overflow their banks. The biggest flood on record destroyed much of Sacramento in 1850.

If acts of God are not enough, Californians also have to put up with such human-caused disasters as oil spills and riots. Yet few Californians view these risks as reasons to consider leaving. Instead, they'll cheerfully point out that California hardly ever experiences hurricanes, killer tornados, paralyzing blizzards, or volcanic eruptions.

CALIFORNIA CULTURES

Ishi's People

Ishi, last survivor of the Yahi tribe

In 1911, workers at an Oroville, California, slaughterhouse discovered a nearly naked American Indian man who had wandered out of the mountains in search of food. His name was Ishi, he was about 50 years old, and he was the last survivor of the Yahi tribe, which had been exterminated by white settlers.

Two anthropologists, Thomas Waterman and Alfred Kroeber, from the University of California at San Francisco, took Ishi into their care. He learned English and described his lost tribe's way of life to Waterman and Kroeber in detail. Kroeber's wife wrote in her book, *Ishi: The Last of His Tribe*, "Ishi was the last wild Indian in North America, a man of Stone Age culture subjected for the first time when he was past middle age to twentieth-century culture." The scientists persuaded the university to provide Ishi with a home at its Museum of Anthropology, where he lived for the rest of his life.

Vanishing Indians

Euro-American diseases and the U.S. Army nearly wiped out California's indigenous population

Today, Native Americans make up less than 1 percent of California's population. Yet when the first Spanish missions were built in California in the late 1700s, an estimated 300,000 indigenous people were living there in 105 tribes, all speaking different dialects. The largest tribes included the Chumash,

Costanoan, Esselen, Gabrileño, Hupa, Juaneño, Maidu, Miwok, Modoc, Pomo, Salinan, Wintun, Yana, Yokut, Yuri, and Yurok. If these tribal names sound unfamiliar, it is because none of them survived into the 20th century.

About one-half of California's native population died from smallpox, measles, and other "white man's sicknesses" within sixty years after the first Spanish expeditions arrived. Many others—nearly 60,000 in all—converted to Catholicism and took Spanish surnames. When mountain man Jedediah Smith arrived in California in 1826, the 150,000 Indians still accounted for 98 percent of the territory's population.

But the Gold Rush spelled doom for most tribes. White settlers feared their Indian neighbors and routinely mounted citizen posses to massacre them. After a series of violent Indian revolts, the U.S. Army began a campaign to eliminate the "Indian problem," culminating in 1872 with the deadly Modoc War. When the Indian wars ended, only one-tenth the number of native people who had lived in California at the start of the Gold Rush survived. The 17,000 remaining Indians amounted to only 3 percent of the state's population.

California's Indians Today

Today, most Native Americans who live in California have moved there from other parts of the country. In the 1970s and '80s, thousands of Navajo people from the huge reservation in Arizona moved to the Los Angeles area to take jobs in the construction trades. Navajo workers are known for their ability to work atop skyscrapers without fear of the dizzying heights.

About 39,000 Native Americans live on reservations in California. The largest include the Hoopa Valley Reservation near Redwood National Park, the Tule River Reservation near Sequoia National Park, and a series of four desert reservations along the Colorado River on the Arizona state line. There are 22 smaller reservations in the area west of San Diego.

Bob Yarbrough/San Diego Convention & Visitors Bureau

Indian dancers

California's Cultural Kaleidoscope

California is one of only three U.S. states that do not have a majority of residents of similar racial origin. (The others are New Mexico and Texas.) Every Californian belongs to one "minority" or another, creating a rich cultural tapestry.

The biggest reason California has become so multicultural is immigration. In 1992, one-third of all newcomers who entered the United States stated that they intended to live in California. The largest groups of immigrants came from Mexico and from the Pacific Rim nations. In recent years, Southern California has also become home to, among others, the largest Iranian and Armenian communities in the United States.

While immigration reached its highest levels ever in the 1980s and '90s, the roots of Hispanic and Asian cultures reach far back into California history.

Hispanic Heritage

San Francisco, Los Angeles, Monterey, Pasadena, San Luis Obispo, Sierra, Nevada, Santa Fe Springs . . . So many California cities and towns have Spanish names that visitors are constantly reminded of the state's Spanish colonial origins.

Since California was part of Mexico until 1848, you might think that much of the state's Hispanic population would be descendants of early-day Spanish settlers. In fact, however, the non-

Indian population of California reached only about 3,000 during the Spanish colonial period. Within ten years after the first pioneers from the United States reached California in the early 1800s, the Anglo population exceeded the Hispanic population. Persecution and victimization quickly drove most Hispanics to move to Old Mexico, so that by 1900, Hispanics accounted for only 2 percent of the state's population.

Today, one out of every four Californians is of Hispanic descent. The growth of the Spanish-speaking community began in the early years of the 20th century, when the U.S.-Mexican border was open with no immigration restrictions. As Los Angeles grew, it offered more and more jobs for newcomers from Latin America. As the Hispanic community grew, so did resentments. Following the Zoot Suit Riots in 1943, the public pressured legislators to pass laws preventing Mexicans from moving to California.

From 1951 to 1964, although immigration was restricted, millions of Mexicans came to California as migrant workers under the *bracero* program, and many stayed in the Los Angeles area. After 1964, border laws became more restrictive, and since that time a succession of tougher and tougher federal laws has made it more difficult for Latin Americans to enter the country legally. At the same time, federal amnesty provisions have made U.S. citizenship available to undocumented immigrants who have lived here for a long enough time. Today, Los Angeles has the largest Spanish-speaking population of any city north of Mexico City.

Some residents' resentments against their Hispanic neighbors still cause tensions in Southern California. Governor Pete Wilson charges that Mexicans who are in California illegally number about 2 million and cost the state more than $1 billion a year.

Labor organizer Cesar Chavez

Despite the intolerance of a vocal few, California has become one of the first officially bilingual states. All legal and public documents are required to be written in both English and Spanish, and schools must make classes available in both languages.

Asian Americans

One out of ten Californians is of Asian ancestry. This amounts to one out of every three Asians in the United States.

Underwood Photo Archive

Many Chinese immigrants started successful businesses in San Francisco

The earliest wave of Asian immigration came during the Gold Rush era, when China was plagued by war and famine, and American brokers brought thousands of refugees to the United States as cheap labor. Most widely remembered for their work on California's first railroads, many Chinese immigrants also became merchants. Prejudice against the Chinese in California was so strong, however, that it forced the immigrants into Chinatown districts in San Francisco and Los Angeles. Today, traditions brought from China more than a century ago are kept alive in these districts. Prejudice also prompted the passage of federal laws prohibiting Asian immigration.

Japanese immigrants also came to California in large numbers at the same time but, unlike the Chinese, most preferred to build rural farming lifestyles for themselves. During World War II, Japanese Americans from California were taken from their homes and put in internment camps around the western United States. While many returned to California after the war, the state's Japanese population has never regained its pre-war level.

Laws against Asian immigration were finally lifted in 1965. California's Asian community, which had not grown significantly during the 20th century, skyrocketed in the 1970s and 1980s to 300 percent of its previous level. Koreans made up the first wave of new immigrants to California, settling in many areas of Los Angeles. Southeast Asian

Michael Leonard Creditor/San Diego Convention & Visitors Bureau

Japanese American taiko drummers

newcomers—Cambodians, Vietnamese, and Laotians—arrived as refugees in the 1970s to settle in both Los Angeles and San Francisco.

African American Californians

Blacks have played roles in California history for centuries. In the 1500s, British explorer Sir Francis Drake had three men and one woman of African descent in his crew. A number of Spanish soldiers who came to California with the Sacred Expedition in the 1700s were black.

California was admitted to the Union as a free state, meaning that residents could not own slaves. The tough 1850 federal Fugitive Slave Law, which was enacted in the same legislation as California's statehood, provided that runaway slaves found in California had to be turned over to their rightful owners. In spite of this law, thousands of blacks came with the Gold Rush. Some came as runaways, struck pay dirt, and negotiated to buy their freedom from their former owners. Others came as slaves of white prospectors. In 1851, a woman named Biddy Mason who had come to California as a slave won a landmark court ruling that if a slave owner stayed in a free state for three years, he lost his property rights in the slave. The court decision meant freedom for as many as a thousand blacks in California. Biddy Mason used her newfound freedom to become a nurse, a real estate developer, a philanthropist, and a local folk hero in San Bernardino, where she spent the remaining 40 years of her life.

In the wake of the Watts Riots in 1965, many blacks in California followed the lead of such political activists as Bobby Seale, Eldridge Cleaver, Huey Newton, and Angela Davis. Others took action in the political arena: Tom Bradley was elected mayor of Los Angeles, Lionel Wilson mayor of Oakland, and Mervyn Dymally lieutenant-governor of the state. In 1981, Allen E. Broussard became the first black justice on the California Supreme Court.

Brobeck, Phleger & Harrison

Former Los Angeles mayor Tom Bradley

Nonethnic Subcultures

Despite a long history of discrimination and racial violence, California has a reputation as one of the most tolerant places in the U.S. It is a rich tapestry of subcultures, not all of them based on race, language, or national origin.

Okies

National Archives and Records Administration

Dust Bowl farmers headed west to the promised land of California

Much like the Mexican *braceros* of a later era, thousands of farmers came from Oklahoma and other states during the Great Depression after losing their Dust Bowl farms to drought. They fled poverty but found exploitation at the hands of large California landowners. John Steinbeck described their plight in his Pulitzer Prize-winning novel, *The Grapes of Wrath*. From old-time religion to country-western music, today's Okies (a formerly pejorative term that became a source of pride in the 1970s) have shaped their own distinctive way of life in Central California.

The Okie capital of California is Bakersfield. Founded by visionary Thomas Baker as part of his plan to dig a 320-mile ship canal linking Kern Lake with San Francisco Bay, Bakersfield has been one of the United States' fastest-growing cities in recent years. Between the 1980 and 1990 censuses, its population increased by 65.5 percent. Country singer **Merle Haggard** not only hails from Bakersfield but, after his hit song, "(I'm Proud to Be an) Okie from Muskogee," brought him fame and fortune, chose to continue living in the blue-collar Bakersfield suburb of Oildale. Bakersfield has fewer tourist attractions per capita than nearly any other California town, and Bakersfield residents like it that way.

Gay and Lesbian Communities

Foremost among these distinctive nonethnic subcultures is the Golden State's lavender community. For the past forty years, California has been home to more gay men, lesbians, and bisexuals than any other state. Beginning with the beatnik era of the 1950s, San Francisco gained a reputation for tolerating unconventional lifestyles. In a time when homosexuals were persecuted in most parts of America, San Francisco was among the few places where gay people could "come out"; thousands of men moved here from all over the country.

San Francisco still boasts the largest gay community in the United States. Homosexuals have become a major political and social influence in local politics. In 1977, Harvey Milk became a San Francisco City Supervisor, the first publicly declared gay man to hold a major municipal office in any U.S. city. He was assassinated a year later, along with the mayor, by a homophobic political opponent. Since then, there has always been at least one gay City Supervisor. Despite the dreadful toll of the AIDS epidemic, official estimates claim that one out of seven San Francisco residents is gay.

San Francisco's two main gay districts are along Polk Street between downtown and Fisherman's Wharf, and along Castro Street on the city's south side. Together, the two areas have more than 200 gay nightclubs, many of which feature outrageously glitzy shows. Straight patrons are welcome at many, though not all, clubs for a firsthand glimpse into this important California subculture. Less adventurous visitors may enjoy strolling along Polk Street and checking out the many Victorian antique shops and chic fashion boutiques along the way.

Rick Gerharter

Tens of thousands turn out for San Francisco's yearly Gay Pride march

Gay and lesbian communities thrive in many other California cities, too. The East Bay—Berkeley and Oakland—is something of a lesbian mecca, as are the smaller communities of Santa Cruz and Eureka. In the wine country, gay vacationers from the Bay Area and elsewhere congregate in the little resort town of Guerneville. And West Hollywood has the largest gay population in the Southland, with other enclaves in the San Fernando Valley, Laguna Beach, and San Diego.

BUILDING CALIFORNIA

Spanish Missions

The Sacred Expedition set out from the outpost of Loreto in Baja California in 1769 under the spiritual leadership of Father Junipero Serra. The expedition also included 300 Spanish soldiers, half of whom died on the journey, and herds of livestock. Its purpose was to convert the indigenous people of Alta California (which is now the U.S. state of California) to Catholic Christianity.

Bob Yarbrough/San Diego Convention & Visitors Bureau

Mission San Luis Rey

In a land where the Indians lived in huts and temporary shelters, the mission churches were the first permanent structures ever built. Father Serra completed construction on nine missions before his death. Besides the church, each mission contained dining rooms, living and work areas for the priests, libraries, hospitals, and cemeteries. They also held vast expanses of land. Santa Barbara Mission, for example, used 122,000 acres as vegetable gardens, orchards, vineyards, and pastures.

The missions established by Father Serra were San Diego de Alcalá (1769, at the site of modern-day San Diego), San Carlos Borromeo (1770 at Carmel), San Antonio de Padua (1771 near King City), San Gabriel Arcángel (1771 at San Gabriel), San Luis Obispo de Tolosa (1772 at San Luis Obispo), San Francisco de Asís (1776 at San Francisco), San Juan Capistrano (1776 at San Juan Capistrano), Santa Clara de Asís (1777 at Santa Clara), and San Buenaventura (1782 at Ventura). Serra's successors built 12 more missions over the next forty years, including those for which the modern cities of Santa Barbara, Santa Cruz, Soledad, San Jose, San Juan Bautista, San Miguel, San Fernando, and San Rafael were named.

The conversion of California's Indians got off to a slow start. During Father Serra's lifetime, each mission averaged only about forty new converts a year. At the time of his death, only one out of 400 Indians in California had become a Christian. Over the next two generations, however, the number of "Mission Indians" grew to about 60,000—more than one-third of all the Indians in the state—controlled by only 60 priests and 300 soldiers.

Soon after Mexico won its independence from Spain, the new government banished the Catholic clergy, and the governor of California sold the missions to private landowners. When California became United States territory after the Mexican War and the missions were returned to church ownership, many had fallen into a sad state of disrepair. Roofs caved in, stucco cracked, adobe walls melted into mud, and campaniles and pilaster windows crumbled away. It was not until 1903 that the California Historic Landmark League first undertook to restore the missions.

Of 21 original missions, 11 have been restored. All are open to the public as museums, and a few are also used for church services. The most interesting missions to visit include **Mission San Juan Capistrano**, the oldest Spanish mission still standing in California; **Mission Santa Barbara**, the centerpiece of one of California's most attractive cities; **Mission La Purisima Concepción**, where carefully detailed restoration brings the Spanish mission era alive; and **Mission San Antonio de Pala**, the only mission still used by Native Americans, on the Pala Indian Reservation near San Diego.

Today, Father Junipero Serra's statue stands beside that of George Washington in the United States Capitol in Washington, D.C. Serra has been nominated for sainthood in the Catholic Church.

California Office of Tourism

Mission San Carlos Borromeo in Carmel

Historic Districts

San Diego's former red-light district now houses art galleries

The idea of historic preservation originated in California decades before other states realized that old buildings were anything more than eyesores. California's most interesting historic districts include:

San Diego's **Old Town** was the site of the original 18th-century Spanish mission and settlement established by the Sacred Expedition. Spanish colonial buildings, restored or rebuilt as part of Old Town San Diego State Park, share romantic Old California atmosphere with shops and cafés. Rangers guide free daily tours. ***FYI:*** Park Headquarters, 4002 Wallace Street; 619-237-6770.

More than 100 buildings in the **Gaslamp Quarter**, San Diego's downtown center in Victorian times and later a red-light district, were revived to become one of the U.S.'s largest historic districts. Today, most San Diego art galleries are located here.

Within walking distance of downtown L.A.'s Union Station, **El Pueblo de Los Angeles State Historic Park** preserves historic buildings dating back to the 18th century, including the Avila Adobe, L.A.'s oldest building. Olvera Street, the district's hub, offers taco stands, import shops, and ersatz Old Mexico charm.

Santa Barbara's Red Tile Route guides visitors through a downtown historic district that was mostly demolished and redeveloped after a 1925 earthquake. A Spanish military post and chapel are preserved at **El Presidio de Santa Barbara State Historical Park**. Colonel John C. Fremont used one early 19th-century home on the route as headquarters when his army captured Santa Barbara during the Mexican War. ***FYI:*** Park Headquarters, 136 East de la Guerra Street; 805-966-1601.

Another exceptional historic walking tour is Monterey's **Path of History**. Starting from Fisherman's Wharf, the 14-block walk shows off various 19th-century Mexican and American architectural styles; the spot where the U.S. flag first flew over California; a typical Spanish Colonial-era herb and vegetable garden; California's first theater; and a house once occupied by author Robert Louis Stevenson.

Despite its rich heritage as California's largest city (until the 1920s) and its Victorian "painted lady" homes, San Francisco offers surprisingly little in officially designated historic districts—mainly because so many buildings were irreparably damaged in the 1906 earthquake and fire. The original Mission San Francisco de Asís, the city's oldest building, endures in the shadow of a larger modern basilica in the **Mission District**.

James Blank/San Diego Conv. & Visitors Bureau

Balboa Park, spanning over 1,000 acres, is the cultural hub of San Diego. Within its borders are gardens, museums, art galleries, theaters, sports facilities, and the San Diego Zoo.

San Francisco's **Presidio**, built in 1776 and used as a Spanish, Mexican, and U.S. Army base for over 200 years, recently became a National Park Service historic landmark. Besides old military buildings now housing museum exhibits, Presidio grounds include 1,500 parklike acres laced with hiking trails.

Old Sacramento, a 28-acre national historic landmark near the state capitol, features over 100 Gold Rush-era sites, including an ornate 1849 theater, a schoolhouse, a sailing ship that once carried goods up the Sacramento River, and the California State Railroad Museum.

The Sierra Nevada teem with gold-mining towns so authentic that several have been movie locations, from *High Noon* to *Back to the Future III*. The best Gold Rush-era town is **Columbia**, a tiny community that once came within two votes of becoming California's state capital. The entire town is a state historic park.

Craig Buchanan/San Francisco Conv. & Visitors Bureau

San Francisco's diversity extends even to styles of Victorian architecture

Another Historic Landmark

The **McDonald's** fast-food chain started in a small Fresno drive-in restaurant in 1950. If you're near Fresno, why not stop for a bite, if only so you can tell friends that you ate at the first McDonald's? It's at Blackstone and Shields avenues.

Manmade Oddities

Cabot's Indian Pueblo, a 35-room, four-story Hopi-style structure in Desert Hot Springs, was built single-handedly by early settler Cabot Yerxa over a 20-year period. Formerly Cabot's private home, the pueblo contains an art gallery, trading post, and museum of Indian artifacts and pioneer memorabilia. (Note: The Hopi people never actually lived in California.) ***FYI:*** East Desert View Avenue, Desert Hot Springs; 619-329-7610.

While we're on the subject, though, an allegedly ancient Hopi legend holds that before the first Indians came, the Southwest was inhabited by a race of Lizard People who lived in underground cities. One city, they say, was beneath downtown Los Angeles. In the 1930s, civil engineer Warren Shufelt organized a massive excavation project seeking entrance into the Lizard People's tunnels. Although he found nothing, the legend has persisted for generations, resurfacing each time a construction crew finds one of the mysterious tunnels that, it seems, actually do exist beneath the city. Large enough to drive a car through, the tunnel network runs from downtown L.A. to old Chinatown (now Koreatown) and were probably made by early Chinese immigrants who feared traveling the surface streets. Tours through the tunnels around Olvera Street are led by a group of docents called Las Angelitas.

One of L.A.'s most visible landmarks, the HOLLYWOOD sign in the Hollywood hills, was erected in 1923 to promote a housing development; it read "HOLLYWOODLAND" until 1949. Each white sheet-metal letter is 30 feet wide and 50 feet high. A hiking trail leads to the sign from Durand Drive near Beachwood Drive.

Palm Springs Tourism

More than 4,000 electricity-generating windmills are a striking sight outside Palm Springs

Los Angeles cigarette manufacturer and visionary Abbot Kinney bought a desolate tidal flat south of Santa Monica in 1904 and subdivided it, modeling his new community after romantic Venice, Italy. He built the 16-mile **Venice Canals** and operated a public transportation system of gondolas. Unfortunately, the canals interfered with oil drilling and were eventually abandoned. Today, some canals have been resurrected and gondolas once again glide past Italianate villas. ***FYI:*** Venice Gondola Charters, 4016 Lyceum Avenue, Venice; phone 310-823-5505.

The biggest, most costly machine you may ever see is the **Stanford Linear Accelerator** on the Stanford University campus in Palo Alto. The multibillion-dollar atom-smasher is 2 miles long and covered with LED displays, control panels, and recording devices. Scientists scurry around doing whatever it is that people who study subatomic physics do, and you can watch them do it on a two-hour tour. ***FYI:*** 2575 Sand Hill Road, Palo Alto; 415-926-2204.

Manmade lakes are found wherever a river flows down from the mountains, but the **Salton Sea** is something else. It's an "inland sea," a large body of water with no outlet. The 1,325-square-mile sea was accidentally created in an Imperial Valley dry lake bed known as the Salton Sink. The lake bed lay 235 feet below sea level, under sun so hot and rain so scarce that any accumulated water evaporated instantly. But all that changed when civil engineer Charles Rockwood completed the first large-scale irrigation canal to carry water from the Colorado River into the Imperial Valley. In 1905 the river flooded, overflowing the canal and spilling the river into the lake bed. The flood lasted for two years. By that time, the water had filled the whole sink to a depth of 81 feet. Although evaporation lowers the sea's surface a little each year, more than half the floodwater still remains after almost a century, and date palms line the shore. Salton Sea State Recreation Area (619-393-3052) has a boat ramp and beach; elsewhere on the lakeshore the Salton Sea National Wildlife Refuge (619-348-5278) is home to more than 350 species waiting for binoculars to be aimed their way.

Stanford Linear Accelerator/U.S. Department of Energy

Cross-section of the Stanford Linear Accelerator Center's Large Detector, in which electrons and positrons collide

California's Castles

Grandiose mansions, often in the middle of nowhere, are a California tradition. Touring them and vicariously thrilling to the limitless wealth that went into their construction has become a popular California pastime.

Some were built as vacation homes, such as the **Wrigley Mansion** (now an exclusive bed and breakfast inn) on Santa Catalina Island, where the Chicago chewing-gum tycoon spent his summer holidays. The opulent **Huntington Library** in San Marino, originally the home of power-company magnate Henry E. Huntington, now houses one of the finest rare-book collections in America, including 49 original Shakespeare folios and quartos. A multimillion-dollar art collection and 200 acres of gardens also make it worth visiting. Others, such as the lavish Roman-style villa in Malibu that houses the fine Greek and Roman collections of the **Getty Museum**, were never lived in.

One of the most intriguing California mansions, and certainly the most remote, is **Scotty's Castle** in Death Valley National Monument. Completed in 1933, the huge, neo-Spanish hacienda with its sumptuous interior decor was the home of Walter Scott, better known as Death Valley Scotty. According to legend, the source of Scott's wealth was a secret gold mine in the desert. In truth, however, Scott's secret was that he was merely housesitting the castle for its real owner, Chicago millionaire Albert Johnson, who rarely came to visit because the house was so hard to get to. ***FYI:*** Tour reservations are necessary, especially on weekends; 619-786-2392.

Another amazing abode is the **Winchester Mystery House** in San Jose. It was built in 1880 by Sarah Winchester, the heiress to the Winchester firearms fortune. A spiritualist who not only believed in ghosts but wanted her home to provide a habitat for them, she convinced herself that she would not die before the house was finished. So she never finished it, but kept adding more and more rooms in a bewildering assortment of architectural styles, secret passages and

Winchester Mystery House

Sarah Winchester couldn't stop adding on

mazelike dead-end hallways. She died anyway in 1922, when the house had been under construction for 38 years. The house, which is open to the public, contains 160 rooms and covers 6 acres. ***FYI:*** 525 South Winchester Boulevard, San Jose; 408-247-2101.

California Parks & Recreation Dept.

Media mogul William Randolph Hearst

But when it comes to mansions, few places on earth can compare to **Hearst Castle**, the 165-room palace of publishing magnate William Randolph Hearst above the coastal village of San Simeon. The Hearst Castle is the second most popular sightseeing attraction in California, surpassed only by Disneyland. Throngs of visitors come to gaze in disbelief at the ostentatious surroundings—the priceless tapestries, carpets, candelabra, furnishings, and even fireplaces that Hearst bought from the grand old estates of Europe after World War I and carried to his ranch by wagon—5 tons at a time. There is even a gold-plated swimming pool, not to mention the zebras, Barbary sheep, and other semiwild offspring from Hearst's private zoo that still roam the grounds. Hearst lived there for 28 years but never considered the castle complete, extending it each year with additions in a bewildering variety of architectural styles. After his death in 1951, the family tried to sell the estate, but even the wealthiest Hollywood tycoons balked at the $50 million asking price and $9,000-a-day housekeeping expenses. The Hearsts finally unloaded the castle on the state parks department in exchange for a massive tax write-off; the family still owns 60,000 acres of land adjoining the castle grounds. ***FYI:*** Tour tickets must be bought in advance; 800-444-7275.

California Parks & Recreation Dept.

Main library at the Hearst Estate

California by Rail

Trains are central to California history. Before railroads, people estimated time of day and set town clocks by the sun's shadow—stagecoach passengers arriving in a new town always had to reset their watches. Regular train schedules required separate towns to agree on the time of day, so Pacific Standard Time was born.

The Bettmann Archive

Chinese laborers made up 90 percent of the Central Pacific Railroad work crews

The Octopus

The railroad came to California in 1861 through an association of "robber barons" known as the Big Four—Charles Crocker, Mark Hopkins, Collis P. Huntington, and Leland Stanford—who conceived and built the Central Pacific Railroad. From Sacramento, Chinese workers laid track over the Sierra Nevada, across Nevada's barren desert and Utah's salt flats, to meet the Union Pacific Railroad at Promontory, Utah.

The railroad opened Eastern U.S. markets to California's Central Valley farmers, allowing the large-scale industrial farming that characterizes the Central Valley today. It also opened California to waves of newcomers. The Southern Pacific Railroad, another Big Four enterprise, linked San Francisco and L.A. with interstate railroads; its 1877 arrival in L.A. enabled growers to ship citrus fruit throughout the country.

Unfortunately for farmers, the profits went into the Big Four's pockets. Also known as "the Octopus," the Four controlled most transportation to and from California, and absolutely controlled state government until 1910. The federal government finally broke the monopoly, but only after the Octopus had sold out to another tycoon.

The Scenic Route

One excellent way to enjoy Southern California's magnificent coastline is aboard **Amtrak**'s *Coast Starlight*. The train passes Malibu; climbs barren, rocky mountains to reach Santa Barbara; crests San

Luis Obispo's pastoral hills and enters Salinas, the artichoke capital of the world; then reaches Oakland after dark, where a shuttle connects into San Francisco. As the northbound train leaves L.A. each morning, a southbound train leaves Oakland. More people ride this Amtrak route than any other; make reservations well in advance.

Mass Transit, San Francisco Style

Briton Andrew Smith Hallidie moved to San Francisco in 1852 and developed a cable system to carry freight, such as gold ore, up and down mountains. In 1871, Hallidie realized a continuously moving cable could also take passenger trolleys over San Francisco's steep hills, and the city's legendary cable-car system was born. The cable cars would have been junked long ago, except that their uniqueness generates civic pride as well as tourist interest.

For practical transportation, BART (Bay Area Rapid Transit) is unbeatable. The 75-mile high-speed train system cost bay-area taxpayers $792 million in the 1950s—worth every penny. People leave cars at East Bay BART stations, travel *under* the Bay Bridge's eternal traffic jam (and the bay), and arrive closer to their downtown San Francisco destinations than they could park.

Mass Transit, Los Angeles Style

Considering BART's success, the lukewarm reception given L.A.'s new Metrorail rapid-transit system surprised some planners. The project caused problems early on: L.A.'s agreement to buy high-speed bullet trains from a Japanese manufacturer irked citizens who wanted American-made trains instead. Soliciting new bids, L.A. found no American company that built the trains so bought them from the Japanese anyway.

Partly because of the controversy, the system's 1993 opening attracted few passengers. When the January 1994 earthquake closed many freeways, train ridership tripled to 31,000 passengers within the first week. A month later, however, passengers totaled 16,000, just above the previous level—compared to the estimated 6 million drivers who use L.A.'s freeways each week.

San Francisco Convention & Visitors Bureau

Powell Street cable car descends San Francisco's Nob Hill

Suburbia

In spite of the obstacles posed by its bordering steep mountains, Los Angeles is the hub of one of the world's largest expanses of suburbia. The greater L.A. area includes no fewer than 168 municipalities.

All of these towns, from Anaheim and Long Beach to Burbank and beyond, boomed in the early 20th century, until they blended into a vast mass of development. Instead of small downtowns ringed by residential areas, they became commercial islands in a seamless sprawl of stucco houses with thirsty lawns.

San Diego Convention & Visitors Bureau

Beach culture: suburbia's first cousin

What seems mundane to many visitors today—a nearly endless gridwork of shopping centers, mini-malls, convenience stores, and big, square, metal industrial buildings, all tethered by freeways and boulevards in a sea of neighborhoods where home exteriors are strikingly similar—was an earlier era's miracle of progress. When the motorcar came to Southern California, it brought growth; between 1923 and 1943, Los Angeles County built more than 8,000 miles of limited-access highways that channel drivers to and from the city center.

This advancement, unknown elsewhere in America, was the birth of the California dream. The Model T Ford and its offspring enabled Californians to live out past the city's edge in an affordable house with a yard to mow and room to dream about putting in a pool; to drive to the beach on weekends; and simultaneously to work in the city where good-paying white-collar jobs were plentiful. Nothing like it had been seen in the world before.

Growth spilled over the edge of the Los Angeles Basin, north into the San Fernando Valley, with the coming of Southern California's aerospace industry. Today, the suburban sprawl commonly called "the Valley"—Glendale, Burbank, Encino, North Hollywood, Mission Hills, Valencia, Studio City, Woodland Hills, Sherman Oaks, Van Nuys, and a host of other 'burbs—fills a 177-square-mile area north of Los Angeles and houses more than 1.3 million people.

National Archives and Records Administration

L.A.'s love affair with transportation goes way back. Here, Pickwick stages, 1920s counterparts to modern-day buses, await passengers outside Union Station.

Yet suburbia itself has changed. Rising gasoline prices, tougher environmental restrictions, and the pure hassle of traveling chronically congested freeways have soured the dream of a city on wheels. Today, one survey shows, nearly 80 percent of all Valley dwellers work and shop in their home communities. Only 7 percent of Southern California suburbanites work more than an hour's drive from their homes, a far lower rate than in most large Eastern and Midwestern cities.

While Los Angeles may have invented suburban sprawl, the Southland's residential wilderness has a sleek new rival wrapped around the south end of San Francisco Bay from Palo Alto to San Jose. Nicknamed "Silicon Valley," the area started to grow in the years after World War II, when Stanford University became a center of technological development. Electronics companies such as Hewlett-Packard clustered around the university. Stanford, in turn, encouraged this growth by creating an 8,000-acre electronics industrial park—the first of its kind in the nation—where television, radar, microwaves, and transistors were developed.

The microchip era began in 1957 when Fairchild Semiconductor opened its plant near Palo Alto. Since then, the Santa Clara County population has climbed to five times its previous size, the number of computer-related companies has grown to 2,600, and the county has the highest per-capita income in California. Much of Silicon Valley's continuing growth today is from immigration, as engineers and technicians from Asian nations accept positions in Silicon Valley high-tech companies. Immigrants who declare San Jose as their intended residence in the United States number about 24,000 a year.

Santa Clara Chamber of Commerce

The tiny microchip—smaller than a dime—transformed Santa Clara County into the computer capital of the world

TASTE OF CALIFORNIA

California Cornucopia

When it comes to agriculture, no other state in the country can compare with California. From figs to sugar beets, from cattle feed to the hops used in flavoring beer, California's farm production is unrivaled.

Citrus Fruits

Fresno Convention & Visitors Bureau

Orange groves near Fresno

Oranges are among the first crops that come to mind when we think of Southern California agriculture. The state produces more oranges than any other state except Florida. It also grows three-fourths of the lemons in the United States, as well as grapefruits, limes, and tangerines. The first orange groves, numbering about 400 trees, were planted by Spanish monks at Mission San Gabriel in 1804. Agricultural entrepreneur Jean Louis Vignes began growing oranges in the area that is now downtown Los Angeles in 1834, and the first commercial orange orchards, planted by retired fur trapper William Wolfskill, began operation in 1841. The citrus industry boomed in the 1880s as the coming of the railroads opened vast new markets to California growers. At the same time, growers began cultivating Valencia oranges (which ripen in summer and fall) along with their established groves of navel oranges (which mature in winter), making oranges a year-round crop.

In 1905, orange growers banded together to form the California Fruit Growers Exchange. Forty-seven years later, the name of the marketing cooperative was changed to Sunkist Growers Inc. California citrus fruits can be identified in supermarkets by the familiar "Sunkist" stamp on their peels.

Designer Berries

In 1881 botanist Judge James Logan crossed wild California blackberries with red raspberries. His hybrid species, the loganberry, flourished, producing more fruit per acre than any other berry. The University of California developed a program for distributing loganberry seeds to farmers throughout the state.

Forty years later, Rudolph Boysen improved upon the loganberry by crossing it with a different strain of raspberry. He named the resulting hybrid the boysenberry but did not commercialize it. In 1933, Anaheim farmer Walter Knott "rediscovered" the boysenberry. His berry fields became Knotts Berry Farm.

Boysenberry bushes yield 5 tons of berries per acre!

Other Fruits

It's sometimes said that everything grows better in California sunshine, but this has not always proved true. Around the turn of the century, fruit growers tried introducing apple trees in their orchards, only to find that something about the climate or soil conditions made their apples inferior to those from the Pacific Northwest and other areas of the country. Instead of solving this perplexing problem, growers simply turned their attention to other fruits. Today, few apples are grown in California, but the state's fruit orchards are major sources of plums, grapes, nectarines, cherries, pears, peaches, figs, dates, and melons. California grows 95 percent of all the apricots in the United States.

The most common palm trees in Southern California today are date palms, which were introduced in the 18th century by Spanish missionaries. Commercial date orchards have been cultivated since 1902 in the arid countryside of the Coachella and Imperial Valleys, where virtually all of the dates sold in the United States are grown—about 70 million pounds a year.

The most recent fruit to find commercial success has been the kiwi. Originally known by the unappealing name "Chinese gooseberry," the fruit's name was changed to kiwi, a tribute to its New Zealand origins, when it was introduced to the United States in the late 1970s. Within ten years after the first kiwi fruit appeared in American supermarkets, California was growing more of them than New Zealand was.

Napa Convention & Visitors Bureau

California vineyards produce much of the nation's table and wine grapes

The Man Who Invented Plants

When Luther Burbank moved to Santa Rosa, California, in 1875 at the age of 26, he had nothing to his name but ten potatoes he had brought from his family's farm in Massachusetts. Inspired by Charles Darwin's newly announced theory of evolution, Burbank dedicated the rest of his life to developing new and improved species of hybrid plants. He created more than forty new kinds of plums and ten kinds of berries, as well as new breeds of corn, peas, tomatoes, roses, and poppies. His *New Creations* seed catalogs made him a legend throughout the California farm country at the turn of the century.

Although it is widely assumed that the Los Angeles suburb of Burbank was Luther's namesake, the city was actually named for a local dentist.

Vegetables

California produces more than half of all fresh market vegetables sold in the United States. The state's most valuable crop is the tomato, which adds nearly $600 million annually to the state's economy. About three-fourths of the tomato crop is canned or processed into sauces. The University of California leads the world in studying tomatoes. Scientists there have devised new strains that can be picked by high-speed machines without getting squished, and even a variety that grows square for more efficient packing. The Sacramento River Delta is the heart of tomato-growing country.

California also grows most of the nation's lettuce—$470 million worth each year. The lettuce is grown in dry Southern California valleys using massive irrigation efforts. Often taken for granted, lettuce leaped into the national consciousness in the late 1960s with the efforts of United Farm Workers organizer Cesar Chavez, who won improved conditions for migrant lettuce pickers by rallying a public boycott in support of labor strikes.

California Section, California State Library

Workers packing California pears

Other California-grown vegetables

include artichokes, asparagus, avocados, broccoli, carrots, cauliflower, celery, lima beans, spinach, and squash. The coastal counties of San Mateo and Santa Cruz south of San Francisco produce 90 percent of all the Brussels sprouts in the United States.

Crops in Bloom

Most of the cut flowers sold in the United States come from Monterey and Santa Clara Counties in Northern California and Ventura, Orange, and San Diego Counties in the Southland. A single small area, the Lompoc Valley along Highway 1 north of Santa Barbara, produces almost all the flower seeds in the country.

David Weintraub/San Francisco Convention & Visitors Bureau

Boutiques in San Francisco's Cow Hollow district offer fresh California flowers

New Directions in California Farming

For a while, it looked as if the family farm was a thing of the past in California. Between 1950 and 1982, the number of farms in the state dropped from 144,000 to 80,000. This 45 percent decline was attributed to small family farmers moving off the land as they were bought out by huge corporate farming conglomerates.

In the past few years, though, trends have changed. U.S. Department of Agriculture figures show that the number of farms actually rose slightly between 1982 and 1992 even though the total number of acres under cultivation went down. This fact is explained by tougher environmental regulations and water restrictions that conflict with traditional agribusiness methods.

More and more California farms today are family-run businesses growing organic crops, often gourmet and specialty produce, herbs, and spices, that command higher prices than mass-produced fruits and vegetables do. As widespread groundwater pollution from fertilizers and pesticides is raising concerns about the future of large-scale agriculture in California, many modern farm entrepreneurs foresee "small-is-beautiful" organic farms outliving today's huge, high-tech superfarms.

Public Markets

In the Depression era, **Los Angeles Farmers' Market** was where growers from all over Southern California brought their produce to sell directly to city dwellers willing to drive a ways for fresh fruits and vegetables. Unfortunately, Farmer's Market also became a big tourist attraction. Today, this sprawl of vendors' stands has changed character to become a tacky blend of flea market, carnival, and World's Largest T-Shirt Shop. You can still stock up on fruits and vegetables galore, but instead of coming fresh from the Imperial Valley, most produce is imported from Latin America and costs more than crops off the same boat sell for in supermarkets. Still, the usually crowded market is a traditional California experience—sort of like Disneyland but without the rides. ***FYI:*** 6333 West Third Street; 213-933-9211.

Kevin Sanchez/Sonoma Valley Visitors Bureau

Sonoma Farmers Market

For the real thing, head downtown to the giant **Grand Central Market**, a big warehouse with sawdust floors where truck farmers, butchers, bakers, and fishermen come to sell their wares and everybody from Southern California's top chefs to people who can't afford to shop at the supermarket come to buy. ***FYI:*** 317 S. Broadway; 213-624-2378.

Nearby, the **Los Angeles Flower Market** is where Southern California flower growers bring their blooms. Most florists in the city make daily journeys to the market around dawn to stock up their inventory, but anybody can buy flowers here—at unbelievably low prices. Stalls line both sides of the street, filling the market with blazing color and fantastic bursts of fragrance. Be sure to go early. Most of the activity ends by 9:00 a.m.

Simply because of its vastness, Los Angeles has a wider array of ethnic markets than you'll find anywhere else west of the Big Apple. Seek out any of these places, and you're sure to find foods you've never seen before:

Alpine Market—German, 833 W. Torrance Boulevard, Torrance, 310-327-2483; Bezjian's Grocery—Middle Eastern, 4725 Santa

Monica Boulevard, Hollywood, 213-663-1503; Bharat Bazaar—East Indian, 11510 West Washington Boulevard, Culver City, 310-398-6766; Bay Cities Importing—Italian, 1517 Lincoln Boulevard, Santa Monica, 310-395-8279; Pacific Supermarket—largest Japanese market in the U.S., 1620 West Redondo Beach Boulevard, Gardena, 310-323-7696; and perhaps best of all, Liborio Market—Mexican/Latin American, 864 South Vermont Avenue, Los Angeles, 213-386-1458.

While the open market tradition is strongest in Los Angeles, you can also find great budget gourmet shopping possibilities in the Bay Area. One, of course, is Chinatown, where the Oriental grocery stores, bakeries, and herb shops lining **Stockton Street** are geared more to the culinary needs of local residents than to tourists. A wider selection of Asian food markets is found along **Clement Street** in the Richmond district. Across the bay in Berkeley, Shattuck Avenue's "**Gourmet Ghetto**" features an endless array of specialty food shops as well as perhaps the Bay Area's most complete organic and health food supermarket, the **Berkeley Bowl Marketplace** (2777 Shattuck Avenue, Berkeley; 510-843-6929). You'll find lots of produce fresh from the farm at the **San Jose Flea Market** (12000 Berryessa Road, San Jose; 408-453-1110.)

In the farm country, they still have *real* farmers' markets. They are held weekly, usually on Saturdays. Big markets include the one at **Stockton** and those farther north at **Arcata** and **Eureka.**

Wine Country

Wine is perhaps California's most famous agricultural product today. More than 600 wineries in the state produce more than 90 percent of all the wine in the United States. The winemaking tradition reaches back through two centuries of California history.

Napa Visitors and Convention Bureau

California wineries transform grapes into award-winning wines

Monks grew grapes and made their own wine at most Spanish missions as early as 1798. Mission San Gabriel, for example, produced 400 barrels of wine a year from its vineyards for sacramental and personal use. In the 1830s, French immigrant Jean Louis Vignes started a commercial vineyard at the site where Union Station now stands in downtown Los Angeles. (He was also the first to grow oranges and walnuts in California.)

It was the Gold Rush that really got California's wine industry going, as entrepreneurs saw the roaring business done by saloons in the mining camps. Since it cost much less to grow wine locally than to import alcoholic beverages from the east, crude wineries began springing up in the Napa Valley.

In 1857, Count Agoston Haraszthy de Moksa planted Tokay and Zinfandel grape cuttings he had brought from his native Hungary. His vineyards at Buena Vista, in the Valley of the Moon near Sonoma Mission, were the first fine European varietal grapes in America. Four years later, seeing his success, the California legislature commissioned Count Haraszthy to journey to Europe once more and bring back no fewer than 300 varieties of grape vines that would be used in a program to develop a wine industry in the state, and within three years California

Napa Visitors & Convention Bureau

Wine-tasting is an ever popular Napa pastime

was the third-largest wine-producing state in the United States.

California's wineries have suffered a number of setbacks over the years. In the 1880s, an insect pest called phylloxera appeared on the scene. It ate the roots of grape vines and devastated many vineyards. The war against the phylloxera brought some of the world's leading horticulture experts to California and, with them, a higher level of sophistication in grape growing and wine making.

In 1919, Prohibition put most commercial California wineries out of business. For the next 14 years, the state's old wine-making families kept their varietal grape strains alive on a small scale under an exemption in Prohibition laws that allowed Americans to make up to 200 gallons of wine per family per year—"for personal use." Meanwhile, vineyards saved themselves from bankruptcy by drying their grapes to make raisins. Today, California produces more than 90 percent of America's raisins and 60 percent of the entire world supply.

For a century, wine connoisseurs turned up their noses at California wines, considering them a cheap substitute for the fine vintages produced in France and Italy. In the 1960s, however, when labor activist Cesar Chavez unionized the migrant farm workers who picked grapes in the Wine Country vineyards, rising labor costs made producing California wines as costly as importing French wines, forcing California winemakers to compete on the basis of superior quality. Garnering many international awards during the 1970s and '80s, California wines were finally recognized as ranking among the world's finest.

Since then, the Wine Country has experienced an unexpected boom in tourism. Literally hundreds of wineries offer free tours and tasting sessions. While the best time to visit is in the September-October harvest season, bumper-to-bumper sightseers line Route 29 between Napa and Calistoga on any sunny summer weekend. The quieter Silverado Trail, an old stagecoach route that parallels the modern highway, is the most popular bicycle tour route in the state.

The ceremonial blessing of the grapes is an annual Sonoma ritual

California Eats

Regional and Ethnic Dining

Thanks to the many immigrant groups California has attracted over the years, the restaurants in most cities offer a remarkable range of regional and ethnic cuisines.

California's hungry population meant lots of work for seafood workers, here drying sardines in the sun

In San Francisco, reigning restaurant-scene queen, one essential experience is dim sum in Chinatown. Ancient Chinese dining tradition lets you choose small portions of dozens of dishes from carts that waiters push around the restaurant. One favorite dim sum restaurant is the Hang Ah Tea House (1 Hang Ah Street; 415-982-5686). A hidden treasure frequented by Buddhist students is the low-priced Kowloon (909 Grant Avenue; 415-362-9888.)

You'll find a wide choice of other Asian cuisines in Bay Area restaurants, including some found nowhere else in the country. Vietnamese food is offered at 101 Restaurant (101 Eddy Street; 415-928-4490) in the Tenderloin; try the *bahn joi bo nuong* (spicy beef with lemon grass). Nearby, Phnom Penh (631 Larkin Street; 415-775-5979) specializes in Cambodian food. Sushi abounds in Japantown; try Isobune, where tiny wooden boats carry assorted raw-fish delicacies past diners along a miniature aqueduct, inviting them to sample whatever looks good. Across the bay in Berkeley, are Szechuan, Vietnamese, Indian, and Burmese restaurants, all in a single block of College Avenue.

Los Angeles provides an even wider selection of ethnic restaurants, such as Hollywood's Mongolian Bar-B-Q (5401 Hollywood Boulevard; 213-464-6888) with its buffet-style array of unidentifiable foods; the "Russian avante-garde" Gorky's Café (536 E. 8th Street; 213-627-4060), a famous artists' hangout; or Sheba Cuisine (1437 Third Street #14; 213-576-0536) in Santa Monica, serving authentic Ethiopian food. California's most elegant Japanese restaurant is A Thousand Cranes, in the equally elegant, Japanese-owned New Otani Hotel (120 South Los Angeles Street; 213-629-1200); dinners are in the $100 range. The range of international restaurants in Los Angeles is virtually limitless. Try Argentinian at Gardel's, Armenian and Lebanese at Araz, Australian at Wallaby Darned, Colombian at Los Arrierros, Cuban at Versailles, Hungarian at Hortabagy, Indonesian at JBG's Little Bali, Jamaican at Fama, Moroccan at Koutoubia, or Persian at Shahrzad.

As you'd expect in the city that boasts the largest Hispanic population in the U.S., in Los Angeles you're seldom far from a Mexican restaurant. Extra-special places include these: El Cholo (1121 S. Western Avenue; 213-734-2773), established in 1927, goes beyond the typical tacos-and-burritos fare to serve more unusual Mexican specialties such as tangy enchiladas suizas. La Parilla (2126 Brooklyn Avenue; 213-262-3434), a local favorite in the East L.A. barrio, is so authentic that the waiters don't speak English. Mérida, in Pasadena's historic district (20 East Colorado; 818-792-7371) offers cochinita pibil, poc chuc, and other distinctive Mayan dishes from the Yucatán. The most famous tourist-oriented restaurant in L.A. is La Golondrina (17 Olvera Street; 213-628-4349), serving typical Mexican and American dishes in an atmospheric 150-year-old home; or you can get great Mexican food at a fraction of the usual price from the many taco vendors selling from pushcarts along Olvera Street.

There seem to be more Mexican restaurants in San Diego than across the border in Tijuana. Old Town has dozens, all aimed at the tourist trade, including El Fandango (2734 Calhoun Street; 619-298-2860), with its peaceful patio off the main plaza, and the Old Town Mexican Cafe (2489 San Diego Avenue; 619-297-4330). For traditional Mexican-style tacos at unbelievably low prices, it's El Indio (409 F Street; 619-239-8151) in the Gaslamp Quarter. A venerable old-time movie star haunt is the Mexican Village (120 Orange Avenue; 619-435-1822), where Red Skelton, Liberace, and Ronald Reagan used to eat burritos.

San Diego Convention & Visitors Bureau

Seaport Village restaurant affords spectacular views of San Diego Bay

California Nouvelle Cuisine

Berkeley's **Gourmet Ghetto**—Shattuck Avenue's chic restaurants and gourmet/specialty food shops—originated "California cuisine" (often called California Nouvelle) in the late 1970s. Even though it is internationally recognized, California cuisine is difficult to define, because no two examples are quite the same. The common elements are all-fresh ingredients, highly creative combinations, and small portions designed to be savored, not devoured. Chefs approach California cookery as an art form, paying careful attention to shape, color, and texture, as well as nutrition and taste. With the emphasis on originality and creativity, it's no wonder that today many of the world's great chefs come from Northern California.

Chez Panisse

Berkeley's epicurean delight, Chez Panisse

The most famous Gourmet Ghetto restaurant, **Chez Panisse**, serves fantastic fixed menus, different every night, starting at $60. Reservations are usually required several days in advance. The upstairs café offers slightly less elaborate meals at slightly less intimidating prices. ***FYI:*** 1517 Shattuck Avenue, Berkeley; 415-548-5525.

California cuisine immediately caught on throughout the state. A tour of California's trendiest—and priciest—restaurants might include: Monterey's **Fresh Cream** (Heritage Harbor; 408-375-9798), as sleek and chic as any California eatery; Santa Barbara's **Citronelle** (901 Cabrillo Boulevard; 805-963-0111), the ultimate bistro; the L.A. area's **St. Estephe** (2640 North Sepulveda Boulevard, Manhattan Beach; 213-545-1334), serving nouvelle-style lamb, veal, seafood, and poultry dishes with an American Indian slant and Santa Fe style; **Chinois on Main** (2709 Main Street, Santa Monica; 310-392-9025), the best of restaurant impresario Wolfgang Puck's fine establishments; and in the Palm Springs area, **Cuistot** (73111 El Paseo, Palm Desert; 619-340-1000), serving an eclectic selection of unique seafood dishes in the middle of the desert.

If menu prices at these famous restaurants are intimidating, a surprisingly affordable California Nouvelle restaurant where you can dine like royalty for under $20 is San Francisco's **Stars Café**—

food is prepared by the same chefs in the same kitchen as for super-chic **Stars** next door. ***FYI:*** 555 Golden Gate Avenue; 415-861-4344.

A "Typical" California Cuisine Menu

For starters, how does a salad of watercress, goat cheese, and olives sound, with an appetizer of grilled baby salmon in a Rose Beurre Blanc; or maybe a crab-and-shrimp-stuffed artichoke served with coarse-ground mustard sauce? The main entrée might be veal piccata with lemon butter and capers, capon breast in Valencia orange sauce, or bacon-wrapped grilled quail with piñon nuts. Dessert could be as light as passion-fruit sorbet with blackberries—or as self-indulgent as Grand Marnier double chocolate mousse or cheesecake with raspberry coulis.

Or for Something Completely Different . . .

If you find nouvelle cuisine a bit much, here's another uniquely Californian dining experience. In the 1930s and '40s, "diners" were all the rage, and the most distinctive diners were those found in vintage railroad coaches around Union Station. (No restaurateur wanted to move a train car very far from the tracks.) Most of these old-timers are gone now, but you can see what they were like at the **Pacific Dining Car**. This big steak-and-chile place, one of the city's oldest restaurants, is built around the original railroad car. ***FYI:*** 1310 West 6th Street, Los Angeles; 213-483-6000.

Bay Area visitors enjoy a blast from the past at **Caffe Trieste**, San Francisco's number-one beatnik hangout during the 1950s. Nothing much seems to have changed except that Kerouac and Cassidy don't come around any more. This coffee-and-pastry bar is probably the only place you'll ever see a jukebox that plays opera. ***FYI:*** 601 Vallejo Street; 415-392-6739.

Ed Debevic's

Waitrons decked out in vintage '50s style at Ed Debevic's diner

STATE OF THE ARTS

Literary California: The 19th Century

How Californians Learned to Read

Literary traditions began with early visitors whose descriptive journals introduced the rest of the world to the strange land called California. The genre classic was Richard Henry Dana's *Two Years Before the Mast,* first published in 1840 and still in print today.

With the Gold Rush, literary journals became immensely popular in the entertainment-starved mining camps. Major California writers of the time, including Bret Harte, Mark Twain, Joaquin Miller, and Ambrose Bierce, were first published in *Golden Era* magazine, which debuted in 1852. Harte later became editor of 19th-century California's greatest literary journal, *Overland Monthly.* His Gold Rush stories are preserved in *The Luck of Roaring Camp* (1870). Mark Twain's impressions of California life are found in *Roughing It* (1872). Though he wrote mainly poetry, Joaquin Miller is best remembered for his novel, *Life Amongst the Modocs* (1873).

The Old Gringo

The most enigmatic of California's 19th-century writers was Ambrose Bierce. After serving his apprenticeship with the gold-camp literary magazines, Bierce moved to San Francisco and became a force in the local publishing scene, which was still in its infancy. He was editor of *The Argonaut* and *Wasp,* then joined the *San Francisco Examiner* staff. His often-satirical newspaper writing was gathered in the award-winning 12-volume *Collected Works* (1909-12). But Bierce is best remembered today for his dark side. His horror story collections, such as *The Monk and the Hangman's Daughter* (1892), *In the Midst of Life* (1892), and *Can Such Things Be?* (1893), made Bierce the Stephen King of Victorian-era California. At age 70, Bierce went to Mexico to meet revolutionary leader Pancho Villa. He was never heard from again. His disappearance remains a mystery.

The Good Die Young

Scottish novelist Robert Lewis Stevenson fell in love with Fannie Osbourne, a married woman from Oakland, and moved to California to be with her. Despite the scandal, Stevenson followed her in 1879 from Oakland to San Francisco and then Monterey, where they married; they relocated to Europe the following year. Stevenson described his California adventures in *The Silverado Squatters* (1883). Near the end of his short life, Stevenson collaborated with his stepson, Samuel L. Osbourne, on several novels set in California, including *The Wrong Box* (1889) and *The Wrecker* (1892).

The Pacific Lumber Company

Frank Norris' The Octopus *chronicled the railroad barons' exploitation of California farmers*

Short lives seem to have been the norm for California authors in those days. Novelist Frank Norris achieved fame and fortune with *The Octopus* (1901), a fictionalized exposé of the railroad barons who controlled California and exploited its farmers. A year after the book was published, he died from appendicitis—at age 32.

Jack London, the greatest California writer of the Victorian era, was born in San Francisco, the illegitimate son of an astrologer. After one year of high school, two arrests for vagrancy and socialist troublemaking, and a dozen odd jobs, he caught a steamship in 1897 to join the Alaska's Klondike Gold Rush. He returned to California three years later with no gold but plenty of material for financially successful novels such as *The Call of the Wild* (1903), *The Sea Wolf* (1904), and *White Fang* (1906). He built a mansion/ranch in the Valley of the Moon near Calistoga, where he experimented with organic farming and raised pigs. When the mansion burned to the ground, he fell into a deep depression and was unable to write. He took his own life at the age of 40. The ranch and the ruins of the burnt-out mansion can be seen at Jack London State Park (707-996-2888).

Jack London Library, Glen Ellen

Jack London

Literary California: The Modern Era

Local Writer Wins Prize

Courtesy of the Steinbeck Archives of the Salinas Public Library, Salinas, CA

John Steinbeck in 1962

California's greatest literary figure was John Steinbeck, a Salinas native. Setting most of his novels in Salinas or Monterey farm country, Steinbeck showed many facets of California life: Hispanic life in Monterey (*Tortilla Flat*, 1935); the world of migrant "Okie" farm workers (*In Dubious Battle*, 1936; *Of Mice and Men*, 1937; and Pulitzer Prize-winning *The Grapes of Wrath*, 1939); the Monterey waterfront (*Cannery Row*, 1945, and *Sweet Thursday*, 1954); and the ranch life of his boyhood (*East of Eden*, 1952). Steinbeck won the 1962 Nobel Prize for Literature. Ironically, Steinbeck was branded a "Communist subversive" by agricultural tycoons around Salinas for portraying them as villains in *The Grapes of Wrath*; he was unwelcome in his own home town for most of his remaining life. Community attitudes changed after he won the Nobel Prize; today the town holds a Steinbeck Festival every August. The Steinbeck House and Library is the top tourist attraction in Salinas. But his books—now required reading in most U.S. high schools—are still banned from many central California school libraries.

Other Pulitzer Prize-winning California authors include playwright Sidney Howard for *They Knew What They Wanted* (1924), the late Stanford professor Wallace Stegner for his novel *Angle of Repose* (1971), poet Gary Snyder for *Turtle Island* (1974), and novelist Alice Walker for *The Color Purple* (1982). William Saroyan was offered a Pulitzer Prize for *The Time of Your Life* (1939) but refused it to protest what he saw as the commercialization of his art.

Poems by the Bay

The Beat Movement started in San Francisco around 1956. Although portrayed by the media of the time as a subculture of pot-smoking, promiscuous leftists, "beatniks" turned out to be harbingers of a larger counterculture to come. With little access to conventional media, Beat ideas were expressed mainly through poetry, generating the "San Francisco Renaissance." Lawrence Ferlinghetti, poet and owner of City Lights Book Store, provided a meeting place/performance space for Beat era giants including Henry Miller, Jack Kerouac, Gregory Corso, Pierre Delattre, Gary Snyder, and Michael McClure. Ferlinghetti also founded a small press to publish Beat writers. He was tried and acquitted of obscenity charges after publishing Allen Ginsburg's poetry collection, *Howl* (1956).

Literary arts fell into obscurity in the late '60s as San Francisco's bohemian scene changed from Beat to hippie and psychedelic rock absorbed counterculture poetry. Still, some Beat literary figures, such as Richard Brautigan and Ken Kesey, struck a responsive chord with the hippie movement. Small-press publishing mushroomed in 1960s San Francisco, from underground comix to *Rolling Stone* and *The Whole Earth Catalog*.

Today, the Bay Area remains the undisputed poetry capital of the U.S. Poetry readings are held almost nightly in various San Francisco and Berkeley locations. Long-time San Franciscan Maya Angelou (*I Know Why the Caged Bird Sings*, 1970), selected to write and present a poem for President Clinton's 1993 inauguration, ranks as the most popular poet in the country today. Berkeley poet/publisher Joyce Jenkins' tabloid *Poetry Flash*, distributed free in the Bay Area, is the most widely read poetry publication in the English language.

Nancy Peters

Lawrence Ferlinghetti, poet and owner of City Lights Book Store

Faulkner Meets Bogart

Southern Californians write screenplays instead of poetry. Hollywood has seen its share of literary giants. Nobel Laureate William Faulkner, for instance, spent part of the 1940s writing movie scripts. His best-known movie achievement was *To Have and Have Not*, the first film in which Humphrey Bogart and Lauren Bacall appeared together. Faulkner adapted the screenplay from the Ernest Hemingway novel.

Art Outdoors

In California, admiring art is often an outdoor sport. Sunshine and greenery add a tang of unabashed pleasure to sculpture viewing. Stroll through the **Rodin Sculpture Garden** (Museum Way and Lomita Drive, Palo Alto; 415-723-4177) at Palo Alto's Stanford University campus and see the French artist's masterpiece, *The Gates of Hell.* Or linger amid priceless statuary from ancient Greece and Rome beside the courtyard pool of the **J. Paul Getty Museum** (17985 Pacific Coast Highway, Malibu; 213-458-2003), the world's richest museum. Renaissance marble statues stand sheltered by rows of date palms at the Huntington Library and Botanical Gardens (1151 Oxford Road, San Marino; 818-405-2141).

Huntington Library

Centuries-old statues are surrounded by beautiful rose gardens at the Huntington Library and Botanical Gardens

For something more contemporary, check out **California Scenario** (South Coast Plaza Town Center, Costa Mesa; 714-241-1700), a downtown sculpture garden set against a backdrop of gleaming skyscrapers which features steel redwoods, huge granite lima beans, and other tributes to California's unique character by Japanese American sculptor Isamu Noguchi.

But when it comes to sculpture, nothing compares to what you'll find in Simon Rodia State Historic Park. Nestled in a black neighborhood of South L.A., the park is the site of the **Watts Towers.** Rodia, an Italian immigrant untrained in art or engineering, built these 99-foot-tall sculptural towers studded with found objects as an expression of love for Southern California. The construction began in 1921 and took Rodia until 1954 to finish. City agencies entangled him in red tape until he moved away in disgust, never to talk about his masterpiece again. The towers were later restored and reinforced by the City of Los Angeles as a Cultural Heritage Monument. Sharing the park, the Watts Art Center exhibits contemporary African American art. ***FYI:*** 1727 E. 107th Street, Watts; 213-569-8181.

Messages on the Walls

Painting murals on buildings and walls is a favorite California art form. Some murals are created with grant funding. Others are painted for the sheer joy of it. Still others are done in stealth by children of the night to surprise the world at dawn. Some are later painted over; others are preserved as historic landmarks.

Los Angeles CVB/Michele & Tom Grimm

The Venice Beach mural is larger than life

Look for outstanding examples of urban outdoor art in the L.A. beach communities of **Venice** and **Santa Monica**, where about fifty buildings have been turned into works of art. California nature themes are favorite motifs. Watch for a redwood forest, an undersea garden, and whales.

The half-mile-long **Tujunga Wash Mural**, located along Coldwater Canyon Boulevard in North Hollywood, is said to be the world's largest mural. It depicts the pageant of California history from prehistoric times to the present day.

Grand-scale murals also decorate San Francisco's **Mission District**, a mostly Hispanic part of town with a large artist population. Around Mission Street, you'll find dramatic portrayals of struggling workers, Aztec gods, and street people hanging out. Some of the murals reach 40 feet in height. Also among the most spectacular public works of art in San Francisco is the **Chinatown Mural**. Located on Stockton Street between Pacific and Jackson Streets, it is half a block long.

Carol Simowitz/San Francisco Convention & Visitors Bureau

San Francisco's Mission District showcases 200 murals

Unique Museums

There's no place like California for private, special-interest museums that house improbable collections. Here's a sampling:

Matisse's La Conversation *is on display at the San Francisco Museum of Modern Art*

Collection of San Francisco, Museum of Modern Art

San Francisco's **Museum of Modern Mythology** features pop icons from television commercials of yore. Here you'll find the Pillsbury Dough Boy, a life-sized Jolly Green Giant, and larger-than-life images of those Rice Krispies elves, Snap, Crackle, and Pop. *FYI:* 693 Mission Street, ninth floor; 415-546-0202.

The **Cable Car Museum** in San Francisco not only exhibits antique cable cars but also contains the powerhouse for the cable cars that still operate today. Visitors can see how giant engines wind and unwind the cables that pull the city's cable cars uphill like slanted elevators. *FYI:* 1201 Mason Street; 415-474-887.

And don't miss the **Garbage Museum**, between Oakland and San Jose. The 100-foot Wall of Garbage shows dramatically how much garbage Americans generate in a single second—a startling reminder that Californians throw out more garbage per capita than any other people on earth. *FYI:* 1601 Dixie Landing Road, Milpitas; 408-262-1401.

In San Jose, the **Rosicrucian Egyptian Museum** contains the largest collection in the western hemisphere of art objects from ancient Egypt, including mummies and gold jewelry. Even the buildings themselves are re-creations of the temples of ancient Thebes. The Rosicrucian sect, which has been in San Jose since the 1920s, devotes itself to studying how occult beliefs derived from the ancient Egyptians apply in modern life. The complex also includes an arcane science museum and a planetarium. **FYI:** Park Avenue between Naglee and Randolph; 408-287-2807.

The **Museum of Neon Art** in Los Angeles overflows with bright neon tubes shaped into sculptures, many of them in motion, that demonstrate what happens when this technique is removed from the world of commercialism and explored as a pure art form. Also available through the museum are neon sculpture classes and bus tours of the best signs in Los Angeles. **FYI:** 704 Traction Avenue; 213-617-1580.

The art-deco **Max Factor Museum** is devoted to the role of make-up in motion pictures. In addition to a star's-dressing-room exhibit and displays on the development of cosmetics, the museum is packed with photos of movie stars from silent films to the modern era and contains the world's largest autograph collection. Among the artifacts is a toupee worn by John Wayne.

The **Frederick's of Hollywood Museum** exhibits underwear of the stars, from Madonna's bra to Tony Curtis' skivvies, along with a history of the brassiere since its invention in 1910 by a German immigrant corset maker named (no kidding) Otto Titzling. A portion of the collection was lost during the L.A. riots of 1992, when looters ransacked the exhibit. Mercifully, many items were left behind, including the bra worn by Milton Berle on his 1950s television show. **FYI:** 6608 Hollywood Boulevard; 213-466-8506.

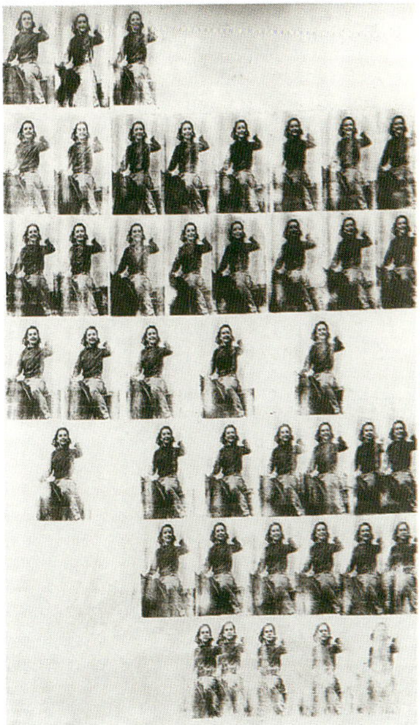

Collection of San Francisco, Museum of Modern Art

National Velvet *by Andy Warhol, at the San Francisco Museum of Modern Art*

Forest Lawn, a 300-acre hillside cemetery in Glendale, was conceived in 1917 as a parklike medley of monumental art and lush landscaping, the most ostenatious graveyard on earth. Over the years, so many classic-era movie stars have been buried there that the place has also become a tourist attraction. Visitors see 1,000 full-size ancient and Renaissance statue reproductions; a giant rendering of Leonardo Da Vinci's *The Last Supper*, the world's largest religious painting; and the tombs of Errol Flynn, W. C. Fields, and Clark Gable and Carole Lombard. **FYI:** 1712 South Glendale Avenue; 818-241-4151.

The Music Recording Biz

Goin' to Surf City

When San Franciscan Al Jolsen went to Hollywood to sing "Mammy" in *The Jazz Singer,* the first musical sound film, its success forged a link between California and the burgeoning record industry. The movies, and later television, offered musicians the kind of money not even Broadway could compete with. Big-name crooners like Bing Crosby and Frank Sinatra made their homes in Southern California. So did serious composers such as Igor Stravinsky and Lotte Lehmann. Musical comedies ranked among the most popular movie genres from the 1930s through the 1950s. Variety shows carried pop singers into the TV era.

But all past history of the music industry in California was eclipsed in 1961, when The Beach Boys—brothers Brian, Carl, and Dennis Wilson along with Mike Love and Alan Jardine—turned America on to the Southern California sun-and-sand scene with songs like "Surfin'," "Surfin' Safari," "Surfer Girl," "Little Deuce Coupe," "Help Me, Rhonda," "I Get Around," "Barbara Ann," and "California Girls." The Beach Boys were inducted into the Rock 'n' Roll Hall of Fame in 1988.

The legendary surf-sound duo Jan and Dean, in their mega-hit California beach anthem "Surf City," lured a generation of adolescent American males westward with the promise of "two girls for every boy." According to the 1990 census, California actually has only 1.016129 girls for every boy. But take heart, guys—the situation improves with maturity. The girl-to-boy ratio is a whopping 2.125 to 1 in the over-80 age bracket!

The West Coast Sound Is Born

The momentum that began with The Beach Boys took on a new dimension in 1965, when the Los Angeles band The Byrds set folk songs penned by Bob Dylan and others to a hard-rock beat, establishing themselves as America's answer to the Beatles with ditties like "Mr. Tambourine Man," "Turn! Turn! Turn!", "Eight Miles High," and "5-D."

The West Coast Sound reached its peak in the late 1960s in the Haight-Ashbury district of San Francisco, where music producer Bill Graham's Avalon Ballroom and Fillmore became the home venues for "psychedelic" rock bands like Jefferson Airplane, Steppenwolf, Quicksilver Messenger Service, Buffalo Springfield, and the Grateful Dead. Classic rock concert posters by Stanley Mouse and other Haight-Ashbury artists can still be found in shops around San Francisco, where they now bring big bucks as collectors' items.

Pop Quiz

More songs have been written about California than any other state. How many of these ditties can *you* whistle?

"California and You" (first recorded by Irving Kaufman, 1914)
"California, Here I Come" (first recorded by Al Jolsen, 1924)
"San Francisco" (Jeanette MacDonald, 1936)
"California Melodies" (David Rose and his Orchestra, 1942)
"San Fernando Valley" (Bing Crosby, 1943)
"Californ-i-ay" (Deanna Durbin and Robert Paige, 1944)
"California Polka" (Tex Williams, 1946)
"Hollywood" (Connie Francis, 1961)
"California Sun" (The Rivieras, 1964)
"California Girls" (The Beach Boys, 1965)
"California Dreamin'" (The Mamas and The Papas, 1966)
"L.A. Woman" (The Doors, 1966)
"California Nights" (Marvin Hamlisch, 1967)
"San Franciscan Nights" (The Animals, 1967)
"San Francisco (Wear Some Flowers in Your Hair)" (Scott McKenzie, 1967)
"California Girl and the Tennessee Square" (Jack Clement, 1969)
"California Soul" (The 5th Dimension, 1969)
"L.A. Freeway" (Jerry Jeff Walker, 1973)
"Hollywood Swinging" (Kool and The Gang, 1974)
"Hollywood" (Boz Scaggs, 1978)
"Hollywood Nights" (Bob Seger, 1978)

Live on Stage

Jim Sharp/Redding Conv. and Visitors Bureau

Folks clap their hands and tap their toes at the Shasta Dixieland Jazz Festival

Music Festivals

One out of every eight concerts and music festivals in the United States is held in California. While top rock and pop acts play to sellout crowds in the Los Angeles and San Francisco metropolitan areas, annual music festivals have become huge events in many California towns, large and small, each summer. Here are some of the best:

April: **Spring Opera Theater**, San Francisco (4 weeks of opera—in English); **San Diego State University Folk and Old-Time Music Festival** (5 days of authentic old-time American folk music)

May: **Ojai Festival** (3 days of chamber music); **Sacramento Dixieland Jubilee** (3 days of ragtime and Dixieland)

June: **Verdi Festival**, San Diego (2½ weeks of opera—in Italian); **Stern Grove Midsummer Music Festival**, San Francisco (10 Sundays of light classical music through early August)

July: **Carmel Bach Festival** (2 weeks of classical music—not just Bach); **Hollywood Bowl Summer Series** (through mid-September, orchestral, pop, and jazz); **Concord Summer Jazz Festival** (2 weekends of conventional jazz); **Music at the Vineyards**, Saratoga (3 weekends in July and August, little-known classical works); **Music from Bear Valley** (3 weekends in July and August, virtuoso orchestral music)

August: **San Luis Obispo Mozart Festival** (6 days, 100% Mozart); **Cabrillo Music Festival**, Aptos (10 days of orchestral and chamber music); **Idyllwild Music Festival** (2 weeks of orchestral music); **San Francisco Symphony Summer Series**, Concord (3 weekends of orchestral music)

September: **Monterey Jazz Festival** (3 days in late September, conventional and experimental jazz)

October: **Western Regional Folk Festival,** Fort Barry (3 days of traditional California songs performed in a natural concert bowl at Golden Gate National Recreation Area)

Performing Arts Centers

Situated in a Hollywood Hills canyon, the **Hollywood Bowl** makes an ideal setting for music under the stars. Shows range from summer light-classical concerts by the Los Angeles Philharmonic Orchestra and the Hollywood Bowl Orchestra to jazz and rock concerts. Admission prices for the orchestra performances start at just a dollar and cost more the closer you sit to the stage. It has become traditional to come early to Hollywood Bowl performances and bring a gourmet picnic.

A classic L.A. outdoor theater of a different kind is found in Griffith Park. The **Greek Theatre**, modeled in concrete after an ancient outdoor amphitheater, was designed with Aeschylus and Aristophanes in mind, but today it is more often used for rock concerts. *FYI:* 2700 N. Vermont Street; 213-665-1927.

Opera has been the mainstay of San Francisco's performing arts scene since the Gold Rush days. Today, the San Francisco Opera is generally considered one of the world's finest, and its annual opening night at the Civic Center's **War Memorial Opera House** is the city's preeminent social event. It is one of 11 professional and amateur opera companies in town. The San Francisco Ballet, which performs at the opera house during the spring and Christmas seasons, is the oldest ballet company in the United States. *FYI:* 301 Van Ness Avenue; 415-864-3330.

THE SPORTING LIFE

Sun and Surf

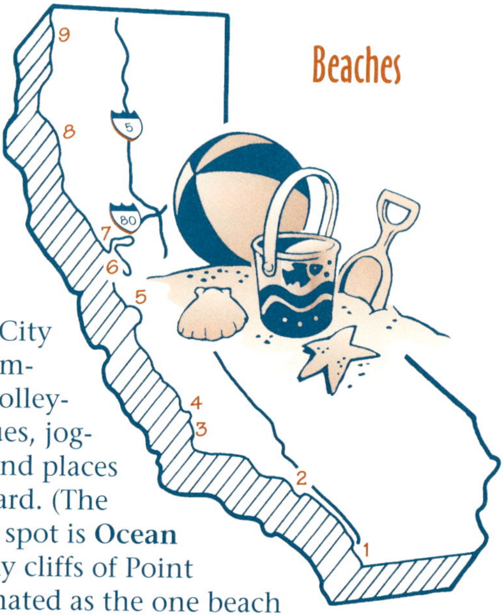

Beachcombing action abounds in California. Here are a few of the most notable spots:

1) Seventeen-mile-long **Mission Beach** and nearby **Pacific Beach** epitomize the lively San Diego beach scene. They're Surf City and hardbody heaven, brimming with rollerbladers, volleyball teams, T-shirt boutiques, joggers, snorkelers, hippies, and places to rent a bicycle or surfboard. (The favorite San Diego surfing spot is **Ocean Beach**, hidden in the rocky cliffs of Point Loma. It is specially designated as the one beach in San Diego where owners can let their dogs run free.)

2) Many of Southern California's weirdest people make their public appearances along the 2-mile boardwalk of **Venice Beach** on the Los Angeles coastline. Street musicians and sidewalk painters, jugglers and bikini-clad roller skaters, more T-shirt shops than you'll find anywhere else in L.A., and a sizeable cross-section of the city's homeless population line the boardwalk. The center of the scene is Muscle Beach, an outdoor weight-lifting area where you can watch the West Coast's top body-builders in action.

3) Point LaSalle State Beach, north of Santa Barbara and Vandenburg Air Force Base, is a remote, gracefully curved beach that's like a vision of paradise (except for the jet fighters that land and take off nearby). It lies on the south end of the Nipomo Dunes, where sand drifts to heights of 500 feet above the surf.

4) At the other end of the 10-mile sand-dune area is **Pismo Beach**, once a mecca for clamdiggers. The Pismo clam is now a rarity, but the water around Pismo Beach Pier remains a popular surfing spot.

5) California's only beachside amusement park, the **Santa Cruz Beach Boardwalk**, has entertained visitors since 1907. The admission-free park features one of the world's top roller coasters, an antique carousel, and 22 other rides, in addition to shops, games, arcades, and Popeye and his family.

6) Make no mistake: the sunscreen and surfboard scene is found in *Southern* California. By the time you follow the coast as far north as San Francisco's **Ocean Beach**, the water is so cold that hardly anyone gets into it without a wet suit. Instead, Northern California beaches are for hiking. San Francisco's Ocean Beach, a narrow black-and-white strand that marks the western shore in the shadow of the urban skyline, is a romantic place to watch the sun set and the city lights rise.

Pismo Beach Convention & Visitors Bureau

Pismo is more popular now for its waves than its clams

7) Stinson Beach, north of San Francisco, is the longest beach in Marin County. Although sharks and cold water discourage swimming, this beach is a favorite among sunbathers and birdwatchers. Nearby **Red Beach**, a local secret, has grottos containing hot springs that can be reached at low tide. It's also Marin County's unofficial public nude beach.

8) The deserted beaches of **Sinkyone Wilderness State Park** are probably the emptiest stretches of sand in the state—and among the most beautiful. This area is called the Lost Coast because it has defied all highway construction efforts. The park is reached by driving 90 minutes on narrow, partly unpaved roads, then hiking as much as a half-mile to the water.

9) At **Agate Beach**, in Patrick's Point State Park north of Eureka, collectors comb the stony shore for agate, jasper, and jade. Sea lions sun on the rocks offshore, and whales can often be spotted from the headlands above the beach during the spring and fall migrations. The park also has a reconstructed Yurok Indian village.

National Archives and Records Administration

Cliff House dominated the beach in San Francisco in 1902

Island Hopping

Rocky, volcanic islands lie off the Southern California coast between Ventura and Santa Barbara. While two are controlled by the U.S. Navy, the other five—San Miguel, Santa Rosa, Santa Cruz, Anacapa, and Santa Barbara—form **Channel Islands National Park**, California's least-visited national park, and provide a remote refuge for unique animal and bird life. The islands also hold the ruins of a Paleolithic American Indian village, one of the oldest archaeological sites in the U.S. The first Spanish explorers found thousands of Chumash Indians living here, though all five islands are uninhabited today. The islands have no developed facilities, and visitors are restricted to marked hiking trails. ***FYI:*** Channel Islands National Park Headquarters, 1901 Spinnaker Drive, Ventura Harbor; 805-644-8262. Guided day trips and overnight camping trips are offered by The Nature Conservancy (805-962-9811) and Island Packers (805-642-1393).

The most famous—and easiest to reach—Southern California island is **Santa Catalina**. Passenger ferries run regularly to Santa Catalina from the mainland towns of San Pedro, Long Beach, Newport Beach, and San Diego, docking at the resort town of Avalon, the island's only settlement. In fact, it is the only resort area on any California island. Avalon's attractions include Catalina Island Museum, Wrigley Mansion and Gardens, a yacht basin, and plenty of intimate, expensive hotels, restaurants, and night spots. Outside the town, the rest of the island is a different world—wild, undeveloped mountains rising 2,000 feet out of the sea, surrounded by rugged shoreline and secluded beaches. Nonresidents cannot drive cars on the island, so the best way to explore is by bicycle. Several streetside stands in Avalon rent mountain bikes. To take a bike outside Avalon town limits, how-

Santa Catalina Island Company

Pleasure craft fill Catalina Island's harbor

ever, requires a $50 permit from Los Angeles County Parks and Recreation (213 Catalina Avenue, Avalon; 310-510-0688). ***FYI:*** Santa Catalina Island Tourist Information Center; 310-510-2000.

California has two other noteworthy islands, both in San Francisco Bay. The larger, **Angel Island**, was a processing station for Chinese immigrants, a quarantine center, and a World War II POW camp before it became part of Golden Gate National Recreation Area in 1972. Today, visitors find picnic areas and hiking trails, including one to the top of Mount Livermore at the island's center.

Santa Catalina Island Company

Catalina's Avalon Bay, with the Casino Building in the background

The bay's other island receives 750,000 visitors every year—yet before 1963, nobody wanted to go there. **Alcatraz**, a.k.a. "The Rock," rises from the middle of San Francisco Bay, where powerful currents and a hypothermic water temperature (45°F) make swimming suicidal and escape virtually impossible. That's why it was chosen as the site for the maximum-security federal penitentiary where Al Capone, "Machine Gun" Kelly, and other famous criminals were sentenced to spend 23 hours a day in 5-by-9-foot cells. After the prison was closed, American Indian activists claimed Alcatraz under a federal law providing for abandoned government lands to be returned to their original Native American residents. After a two-year standoff, the activists were forcibly removed when federal judges decided that Alcatraz was not abandoned because it still had a lighthouse. The U.S. Congress immediately declared the island part of Golden Gate National Recreation Area. Today, a National Park Service concessionaire ferries visitors to the island and guides them through the old prison's bleak corridors. ***FYI:*** Make reservations to visit Alcatraz several days in advance by calling the Red and White Fleet at 415-546-2700.

Top Ten Scenic Drives

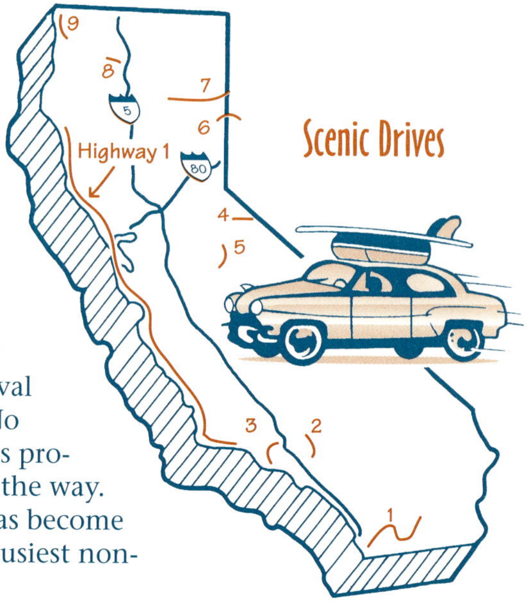

The ultimate scenic drive in California is **Highway 1**, which winds from Santa Monica up the Big Sur coast, through San Francisco, across the Golden Gate Bridge, and into the heart of redwood country. For spectacular scenery, few trips in the world can rival this 600-mile journey. No fewer than 39 state parks provide beach access along the way. It is so popular that it has become one of the California's busiest non-interstate routes.

Motorists seeking open roads, natural beauty, and pure driving pleasure may wish to explore the network of federally designated Scenic Byways that run through the national forests and recreation areas. Here are California's best:

1) Sunrise National Scenic Byway: This 24-mile road climbs from the San Diego area into cool pine forests on the slopes of Mount Laguna, paralleling a section of the Pacific Crest Trail and offering spectacular views of Anza Borrego Desert State Park.

2) Rim of the World: This 107-mile San Bernardino National Forest drive passes popular fishing lakes and the National Children's Forest, where you can walk through an area recovering from a forest fire. From Strawberry Peak Lookout, you can see Santa Catalina, 60 miles away.

3) Angeles Crest Scenic Byway: This mountainous 64-mile trip starts in the Pasadena area, surprising motorists with its quick escape from L.A. traffic into cool mountain wilderness. The road provides access to several ski areas, the Pacific Crest Trail, and the Twin Peaks and Sheep Mountain Wilderness areas. (The latter is home to California's largest population of bighorn sheep.)

4) Lee Vining Canyon Highway: Though only 12 miles long, this road climbs 3,200 feet as it winds from Mono Lake through one of the state's most dramatic canyons to the summit of 9,945-foot Tioga Pass.

5) Sierra Vista Byway: This 100-mile loop road climbs from North Fork to 5,393-foot Mile High Vista in Sierra National Forest for magnificent views of the Ansel Adams, John Muir, and Kaiser Wilderness areas.

Monterey Visitor & Convention Bureau

Scenic Highway 1, along the Monterey coast

6) Carson Pass Highway: From Woodfords, near Lake Tahoe, this 58-mile highway through Eldorado and Toiyabe National Forests crosses an 8,600-foot Sierra Nevada pass and descends to Dewdrop, Nevada, providing access to ski areas, hot springs, and the Pacific Crest Trail.

7) Feather River Scenic Byway: This 130-mile route climbs from the Oroville area through Plumas National Forest to the Nevada state line at Beckwourth Pass. Along the way, it visits historic Gold-Rush-era settlements such as Pulga and Chilcoot.

8) Trinity Heritage Byway: This 111-mile route through Shasta-Trinity National Forest follows the forested shoreline of Clair Engle Lake, the third-largest lake in California, to historic Gold Rush towns like Coffee Creek. Trailheads lead from the road into the Trinity Alps Wilderness.

9) Smith River Scenic Byway: This 33-mile detour through giant redwoods in the Six Rivers National Forest provides access to 17 forest trails and some of California's most luxuriant forest.

Or for a Real Driving Adventure . . .

Try one of the eight rugged, unpaved Bureau of Land Management Back Country Byways—222 miles in all—through the vast East Mojave BLM National Scenic Area. The 1.5-million-acre desert reserve offers Joshua tree forests, giant sand dunes, caves, springs, and the remains of army outposts and stage stations. ***FYI:*** Bureau of Land Management, California Desert Information Center, 831 Barstow Road, Barstow, CA 92311; 619-256-8617.

Golf

Palm Springs Tourism

Golf aficionados flock to Palm Springs' 42 golf courses

Mild winters, reliable sunshine, and spectacular scenery make Southern California an ideal setting for golf courses. The first golf course in California was built at Riverside in 1891, soon after the sport was introduced in the United States. Within ten years, courses were opened at Catalina, Coronado, Los Angeles, Pasadena, Redlands, San Diego, Santa Barbara, and Santa Monica. By 1991, there were over 700 golf cours es in the state.

Most exclusive of all is **Pebble Beach Golf Course**, site of the Bing Crosby Golf Classic, located on a peninsula at the south end of Monterey Bay. This fabulously landscaped seaside course, built by the Del Monte Company in 1900, is now surrounded by some of the most lavish country estates in America on **17 Mile Drive**. Many golfers dream of playing Pebble Beach, but this is a pleasure normally reserved for the very wealthy, as are several other golf courses that surround the community of Pebble Beach today. To feel the thrill of golf at Pebble Beach, make reservations at **Poppy Hills Golf Course**, the public course in Pebble Beach. ***FYI:*** 408-625-2035.

San Diego Convention & Visitors Bureau

Torrey Pines State Reserve, near the Pebble Beach Golf Course

The reigning champion of the California golf resort world, **Palm Springs** supports 42 golf courses in a community of just 80,000 people. Palm Springs, the only city in America ever to elect former pop singer Sonny Bono as its mayor, has been the weekend retreat of the motion picture industry since the 1930s. Former Presidents Eisenhower and Ford built golf getaway homes there. The Bob Hope Desert Classic is held there, as are about 100 other golf tournaments each year.

Go Fish

Sport fishing is popular all along the California coast and upstream all the way to the snowmelt creeks of the Sierra Nevada. The state issues more than 6 million fishing licenses (for salt-water fishing) and anglers stamps (for inland fishing) each year.

Freshwater fishing in the Sierra Nevada is a relaxing pursuit

A fishing license is not required to fish off public piers, and for many people, especially in urban coastal areas, pier fishing provides an important part of their diet. The fish most commonly caught this way are rock cod, calico bass, albacore, mackerel, and halibut. One of the top fishing areas in California is the Sacramento River delta, teeming with bluegill, catfish, perch, striped bass, and sturgeon.

Boaters can head out to sea after salmon, tuna, white croaker, barracuda and, in some areas, sand sharks. In most small coastal towns, it's easy to find fishing guides who will take anglers out to the fishing shoals for as little as $25 a day. In resort areas such as Newport Beach and Avalon on Catalina Island, deep-sea fishing charter boats costing $80 to $100 an hour take sportsmen out in search of marlin and swordfish.

Pristine Lake Siskiyou is a popular getaway

Far more popular even than ocean fishing, however, is trout fishing in the freshwater lakes and streams of the Sierra Nevada. Major areas include Lake Tahoe, Mammoth Lakes, the Kern and Kings rivers in Sequoia and Kings Canyon National Parks. The national forests, especially Stanislaus National Forest north of Yosemite, have literally hundreds of great trout fishing streams. Where to look for good fishing in the national forests depends on which areas have been stocked with trout lately, so it's a good idea to ask at a ranger station for advice before heading into the backcountry.

California Skiing

Skiing in America started in Northern California in the 1850s, when Scandinavian sailors who deserted their ships in San Francisco to seek their fortunes in the gold fields showed fellow miners how to make crude skis (called "snow shoes," though they were more like modern skis than like what we call snowshoes today) from barrel staves.

The Tahoe Snowfest! bunny hits the slopes

Snowfest!

In 1821, Norwegian native John Albert Thompson started a winter courier business in the high Sierra, using cross-country skis to carry mail and parcels to remote mining camps. Towing loads of up to 100 pounds, he took his place in California legend as "Snowshoe" Thompson. He is best remembered for carrying the first ore samples from the fabulous Comstock Lode to the assayer's office.

Everybody in California lives within a few hours' drive of a ski area. In Los Angeles County, about 40 miles from downtown L.A., **Mount Baldy** is one of the most popular ski areas in the state. Nearby in Angeles National Forest are **Kratka Ridge** and **Mount Waterman** ski areas, as well as five cross-country areas.

Farther south, the San Bernardino Mountains reach elevations of more than 11,000 feet. There, such areas as **Bear Mountain**, **Snow Summit**, and **Snow Valley** are great destinations for weekend ski trips from San Diego.

The last place you'd expect to find winter sports is the sun-beaten desert resort of Palm Springs, where people walk around in bathing suits in January. Yet even in Palm Springs, cross-country skiing is a popular pastime at elevations more than a mile above the city in nearby **Mount San Jacinto State Park**.

But the ultimate ski slope that Southlanders can drive to in a day is at **Mammoth Mountain** on the east side of the Sierra Nevada. It ranks as one of the largest and busiest ski areas in the United States.

The popularity of skiing in California and throughout the western United States skyrocketed when **Squaw Valley** was chosen as the site of the 1960 Winter Olympic Games. Today, Squaw Valley is only one of more than a dozen ski resorts around Lake Tahoe. Virtually all of the downhill ski slopes in Northern California—places like **Ski Homewood**, **Sierra Ski Ranch**, **Heavenly**, **Alpine Meadows**, **Northstar-at-Tahoe**, and **Sugar Bowl**—are in the Lake Tahoe vicinity, just three hours' drive from the Bay Area.

Cross-country skiing and snowshoeing trails suited to all levels of skiing ability are the main wintertime attractions in **Lassen Volcanic National Park**. The chance to slide down the side of a volcano also brings out hordes of youngsters for sledding and tubing on a winter sports playground that used to be a downhill ski area before funding shortages closed it down.

National Park Service

Northern California's mountains provide excellent cross-country skiing trails

Sequoia National Park offers the world-class cross-country skiing experience of gliding among the giant redwoods on more than 60 miles of groomed trails from ski touring centers at Lodgepole Village and Grant Grove.

Yosemite National Park's Badger Pass Ski Area, a small downhill slope, is the hub of a system of 90 miles of cross-country trails that runs throughout the park.

Trailwise

The ultimate hiking experience in California—and perhaps in North America—is the Pacific Crest Trail, a 2,400-mile route that follows the summit ridgelines of the Cascade, Sierra Nevada, and San Bernadino Mountains from the Canadian border to the Mexican border. Two-thirds of the trail's length lies within the state of California. Few people have hiked the entire distance, a feat that takes three months and a lot of careful planning. For hikers in search of shorter treks, a number of segments of the Pacific Crest Trail are accessible from main roads. Here's where to find some of them:

1) Lassen Volcanic National Park: The Pacific Crest Trail forms the backbone of the park's 150-mile trail network. The most popular hike here, though, is the 2½-mile switchback ascent to the summit of 10,475-foot Mount Lassen, which erupted in 1915, spewing lava and hurling rock and ash 30,000 feet into the air.

2) Donner Pass: The Pacific Crest Trail meets Interstate 80 at Donner Pass, the site where a wagon train was stranded for six months in the winter of 1846-1847. (To learn how some members of the party survived, thanks partly to cannibalism, check out the Emigrant Trail Museum in Donner Memorial State Park.) From here, the trail follows the ridge line at the top of the Lake Tahoe area ski slopes.

National Park Service

Mount Lassen last erupted in 1915

3) Yosemite National Park: Yosemite is the starting point for the

most popular segment of the Pacific Crest Trail, originally called the John Muir Trail, which runs 250 miles through the alpine wilderness of Sierra and Inyo National Forests to Kings Canyon and Sequoia National Parks. To reach the portion of the trail that runs along the mountain crags of Yosemite, backpackers make a long climb to the crest from the trailhead at Tuolumne Meadows.
4) Devil's Postpile National Monument: The Pacific Crest Trail meets a road again in this eerie mountain landscape of basalt monoliths polished by Ice-Age glaciers into columns 60 feet tall.
5) Kings Canyon and Sequoia National Parks: South of Devil's Postpile, the Pacific Crest Trail runs for 150 miles along the glacial tundra of the High Sierra to its southern tip, traversing the lengths of both Kings Canyon and Sequoia National Parks without nearing a road. Along the way, a short trail branches off and takes climbers to the summit of Mount Whitney, the highest mountain in the lower 48 United States.

Mountain Bike Mania

Mountain biking has grown so much in popularity that it is now among the most popular sports in all areas of California, from the timber roads of Shasta National Forest in far northern California to the stark rock landscapes of the Mojave Desert in the south.

The most popular mountain-biking region in the state is around **Mammoth Lakes** (see 6. on map). Not only is Inyo National Forest laced with hundreds of miles of trails and primitive roads ideal for biking, but in the summer the Mammoth Mountain Ski Area converts its slopes into a one-of-a-kind mountain bike playground. The gondola takes you and your bike to the mountaintop. You can come down along leisurely trails or plunge down the aptly named Kamikaze Trail. ***FYI:*** 619-934-0606.

Shasta Cascade Wonderland Association

Mountain bikers can take their pick of trails throughout California

Ultimate Thrills

Palm Springs Convention & Visitors Bureau

Balloon adventurers take off from all parts of the state

Getting High

All the way up and down the Coast Range, people poise on the crests of hills and the brinks of cliffs for the perfect moment to take flight using **hang gliders**. ***FYI:*** Windsports International, 16145 Victory Boulevard, Van Nuys, 818-988-0111; or Western Hanggliders, Route 1 at Reservation Road, Santa Barbara, 805-384-2622.

Several gliderports offer the swift, silent thrill of riding in a **glider** with an experienced pilot. ***FYI:*** Crystal Soaring, 32810 165th North Street East, Llano, 805-944-3341; or Calistoga Soaring Center, 1546 Lincoln Avenue, Calistoga, 707-942-5000.

Hot air balloons are ubiquitous in California. Balloon adventurers soar high above the desert floor in several eastern California towns, including Borrego Springs, Temecula, and Lancaster, as well as over the spectacular central coast, the Wine Country, the Sierra Nevada, and the Gold Country. ***FYI:*** American Balloon Charters, Palm Springs, 619-568-6700; Balloon Adventure, Lancaster, 818-888-0576; Balloons by the Sea, 71 Myrtle Court, Salinas, 408-424-0111; Airborne of Sonoma County, Santa Rosa, 707-942-5000; Once in a Lifetime Balloon Company, 1485 Lincoln Avenue, Calistoga, 707-942-6541; Mountain High Balloons, Truckee, 917-587-6922; High Sierra Ballooning, Mammoth Lakes, 619-934-7188; or Balloons of Woodland, Woodland, 916-666-6424.

Getting Wet

Scuba diving is practiced along the southern California coast—even just offshore from downtown Los Angeles. ***FYI:*** Marina del Rey Divers, 2539 Lincoln Boulevard, Marina del Rey, 213-827-1131; San Diego Divers Supply, 4004 Sports Arena Boulevard, San Diego, 619-224-3439; or Catalina Divers Supply, Avalon, 310-510-0330.

White-water rafting is popular in many parts of the state, especially on the Russian River and the Stanislaus River. Perhaps the ultimate California rafting experience is down the rapids of Kings Canyon. ***FYI:*** Sierra South Mountain Sports, 11300 Kernville Road, Kernville, 619-376-3745; or Trinity River Company, Big Flat, 916-623-3033.

Kayaking is practiced on both white-water rivers and saltwater bays. One of the most interesting places for sea kayaking is beautiful Monterey Bay. *FYI:* Monterey Bay Kayaks, 693 Del Monte Avenue, Monterey; 408-373-5357.

Surf's Up

Surfing is the quintessentially Californian thrill sport. No other place in North America can claim the number of surfboards per capita you'll find bobbing just off the California coast, patiently awaiting the perfect wave.

Many people believe surfing was invented by Southern Californians to keep them busy through the endless beach hours it takes to keep one's skin bronze-colored. But the truth is, surfing was invented by Polynesians and was first done at Redondo Beach in 1907 by daredevil George Freeth and in Santa Cruz in 1912 by Hawaiian surf champ Duke Kahanamoku.

Surfing did not begin to gain popularity until California Institute of Technology grad Bob Simmons invented a new, lightweight fiberglass surfboard to replace old-fashioned wooden boards. International rules for surfing competitions were adopted in 1966. *FYI:* To learn more about the history of surfing, visit the free **Santa Cruz Surfing Museum**, in the lighthouse on West Cliff Drive (408-429-3429).

Want to watch the world's best surfers in action? **The International Surf Championship and Festival** takes place every August in the Los Angeles area at Hermosa Beach, Manhattan Beach, and Redondo Beach. *FYI:* Call 310-546-8854 for this year's schedule.

Want to try surfing for yourself? Boards are for rent at shops along all top surfing beaches in the Los Angeles area. *FYI:* Zuma Jay Surfboards, 22775 Pacific Coast Highway, Malibu; 213-456-8044.

San Diego Convention & Visitors Bureau

Some of the world's best surfers hit the waves in Southern California

THE SPIRIT OF CALIFORNIA

Love, Hate, and the Automobile

It's no coincidence that Southern California's early 20th-century population boom happened at the same time automobiles became affordable. Unlike eastern and midwestern residents, most Angelenos arrived by car. By 1925, there was one car for every three people in L.A.—more than twice the national average.

Berkeley Historical Center

Ubiquitous California gridlock

Other factors also contributed to Southern California's car culture. America's first automobile club formed here in 1900, and the first state automobile association in 1901. Both lobbied powerfully for road construction throughout the state. California's climate was ideal for pleasure driving in the days when cars had removable tops. As oil wells sprouted, from the first big strike near Los Angeles to vast new discoveries at Santa Barbara, Bakersfield, and San Francisco's Signal Hill, gas stations started appearing around Southern California as early as 1909.

Steeped in the car culture, California originated many motorist-oriented businesses we take for granted today—motels, drive-in movies, supermarkets, fast-food restaurants, drive-up banks, and even drive-in churches. L.A.'s freeway system, the world's first, has shaped the city's development since the 1940s and served as the prototype for all other freeways. Cars achieved their fullest realization as status symbols in Southern California, home of more stock race cars, restored vintage automobiles, hippie vans, sportscars, dune buggies, and neon-lit customized low-riders than any other place on earth.

Californians have also been first to experience the pitfalls of America's automobile

dependence—gasoline shortages, traffic congestion and air pollution. The Southland's notorious "smog" (air pollution) was first noticed in 1947. For a decade, many experts believed the brown air obscuring the skyline to be uniquely Los Angeles' problem—smoke and fog trapped over the city by peculiar air inversions created by surrounding mountains. Only around 1960, when brown clouds started appearing over other U.S. cities, did experts convince the California state legislature that 60 percent of this pollution came from automobiles. That year, the state created its Motor Vehicle Control Board.

Today, air pollution damage to human health and farm crops is officially estimated at $8 million a year, and the greater L.A. area has imposed strict limits on car use. Despite these problems, Angelenos seem reluctant to accept any public transportation system. There is one motor vehicle for every 1.8 men, women, and children in Southern California—Los Angeles County alone has more cars than any other U.S. *state* except Texas. Overall, Californians own 11 percent of the nation's motor vehicles and consume more gasoline than any other state. New laws will force the introduction of solar or electric cars beginning in 1995.

In 1993, experts noticed a change in L.A.-area air pollution patterns. Instead of being worst during weekday-afternoon rush hours as in past decades, today's worst air quality appears on sunny weekends, when city residents hop into their cars and head for the mountains or the beach.

An Old-Fashioned Freeway

America's first freeway, the 6-mile Arroyo Seco Parkway, opened in 1940 to link Hollywood and Pasadena; it later connected to greater L.A.'s planned 1,500-mile freeway system as the Pasadena Freeway (Interstate 210). Narrower and curvier than modern freeways, the Pasadena Freeway with its lush, overgrown landscaping now seems like a quaint relic of an earlier era—an antique freeway. Though bumper-to-bumper during rush hours, in late morning it is refreshingly traffic-free and fun to drive.

In Hot Water

Californians tend to be amphibious by nature. Surfers and sunbathers by the thousands take the plunge along Southern California beaches on any sunny day. Away from the seashore, Southern California boasts more than half of all residential swimming pools in the United States. The Northern California equivalent is the hot tub, which was invented in Marin County and is considered more essential than a television set in many households there. But the ultimate bathing experience in California is to be found in the state's many natural hot springs.

Cammarata & Co. Ltd. Communications

Old Faithful Geyser of Calistoga

Water has been the main industry in the Wine Country town of **Calistoga** since 1859, when San Francisco newspaper tycoon Sam Brannan combined the names "California" and "Saratoga" (a fashionable resort in upstate New York) and built an elaborate spa there. Brannan's original resort is now Indian Springs (1712 Lincoln Avenue), one of several local spas that offer not only hot baths but also massages, volcanic mud baths, and sundry other healthy pleasures. Other resorts in town include Nance's Hot Springs (1614 Lincoln Avenue) and Le Spa de Français (1880 Lincoln Avenue), as well as the New Age-oriented International Spa (1300 Washington Street) and the public geothermal swimming pools at Calistoga Hot Springs Spa (1066 Washington Avenue). Just outside of town, visitors can see geothermal power at full force at Old Faithful Geyser, which spews superheated steam 60 feet in the air.

Among the spas operating today in the Wine Country are **Harbin Hot Springs** (Middletown, 707-987-2477), a holistic resort with massage classes, a vegetarian restaurant, and dormitory-style sleeping arrangements, and **White Sulphur Springs** (St. Helena, 707-963-8588), a country inn-style spa set beside a 300-acre redwood grove.

Other hot springs are found in all parts of the state. During the late 19th century, people would travel thousands of miles by rail to take the waters at now-defunct luxury resorts such as The Geysers at Geyserville, Paso Robles (near San Luis Obispo), Carlsbad near San Diego, and Aetna Springs, which was taken over in 1976 by Rev. Sun Myung Moon's controversial Unification Church.

Today, at **Avila Beach** near San Luis Obispo, visitors can camp on the beach and enjoy the informal resort's seaside hot pools. In the heart of San Francisco's Japantown, **Kabuki Hot Springs** offers communal or private hot baths and traditional Japanese ambience. Perhaps the most restful place in California is the **Tassajara Zen Center** hot springs resort near Carmel. Inyo National Forest around Mammoth Lakes has dozens of natural hot springs pools secluded in forest settings. Locals and knowledgeable vagabonds go there to get naked with nature. The best-known is **Hot Creek Geological Site**; a more secret spot is known as **Wet Willy's** (ask for directions at the National Forest Service ranger station in Mammoth Lakes).

The first geothermal energy plant in the United States was opened in 1922 at the Geysers area of Sonoma County and continued in use until 1985. It used underground steam to drive turbine generators. Pacific Gas and Electric now operates 18 other geothermal power plants in the same area, producing nearly 1.2 million kilowatts of electricity.

Spiritual California

From the headquarters of worldwide sects such as the Rosicrucians and the I AM Foundation to the networks of astrologers, psychic surgeons, channelers, crystal healers, shamans, and UFOlogists studying and practicing in towns all along its coast, California is where the spiritually undernourished can find designer belief systems in every color and pattern imaginable.

In fact, "nontraditional" religions have thrived in California for more than 150 years. Most 19th century sects were utopian; that is, they idealistically sought to organize mini-societies isolated from the society at large. Among those that achieved some fame in their day were the French commune of Icaria Speranza (1881-1886) near Cloverdale, the "Theo-Socialist" colony of Fountain Grove (1875-1892) near Santa Rosa, and the Holy City (1918-1954) near Los Gatos.

Early-day spiritual societies that survive today include the theosophical colony founded in Point Loma by Katherine Augusta Westcott, who was referred to as the Purple Mother; the study center established by East Indian philosopher J. Krishnamurti in Ojai, which is also the location of the Krotona Institute of Theosophy; and the Egyptian-style Rosicrucian temple in San Jose. Sects that swept California in the early 20th century included the Mankind United movement in the 1920s, the Mighty I AM cult of the Depression era, and the Builders of the Adytum, inspired by British black-magician Aleister Crowley.

One of the most famous cults of the 1920s and '30s, which still has followers today, was the Foursquare Gospel movement of spiritualist Aimee Semple McPherson, a forerunner of New Age thought who merged fundamentalist Christianity with reincarnation, free love, and other concepts attributed to the priests of lost Atlantis as interpreted through the French mystic St. Germaine and others. Her popularity spread throughout the world between

1921 and 1926, and she built the huge Angelus Temple near downtown Los Angeles; it cost $1.5 million and seated a congregation of 5,000. She fell into disgrace after a scandal in which she and a lover staged her phony kidnapping, and only the intervention of her friend William Randolph Hearst saved her from a fraud prosecution. Some of McPherson's supporters continued to follow her until her suicide in 1944. The Angelus Temple, modeled after Biblical descriptions of Solomon's Temple, still stands at 1100 Glendale Boulevard.

Of all the cults that have risen and fallen in California, surely the most notorious—surpassing even the Manson family—was the People's Temple, founded by Rev. Jim Jones in Ukiah and later San Francisco. Jones established a utopian commune in the South American country of Guyana and persuaded nearly a thousand followers from San Francisco to move there with him. A year later, after ordering the deaths of a U.S. Congressman from San Mateo and his investigative team who had flown to Guyana on a fact-finding mission, Jones and about 900 followers committed suicide by drinking cyanide-laced Kool-Aid.

William Money (1807–1890)

Scottish-born religious dissident William Money is credited with forming the first religious cult in California. Arriving in Los Angeles at the age of 33, he practiced medicine without a license for more than ten years. After being branded a quack by the medical community there, he organized his own Reformed New Testament Church and declared himself Bishop and Defender of the Faith. His teachings were the subject of the first book ever published in Southern California.

Northern California vs. Southern California

Silicon Valley workers assembling computer components. From e-mail to virtual reality, computers are central to life in Northern California.

Every time election year rolls around in California, you'll hear some politician propose the idea that the state should be split in two, with the state line running through San Luis Obispo, Tehachapi, and Barstow. The idea was put forth for the first time in the Constitutional Congress of 1849 by politicos from Los Angeles, San Bernardino, San Diego, San Luis Obispo, Santa Barbara, and Tulare; the split was vehemently opposed by Northern Californians. Most recently, in 1992, a bill to split the state was espoused by Northern Californians seeking to slow the draining of their water and power resources by the Los Angeles megalopolis; Southern Californians voted it down.

So different is California's Southern "yin" from its Northern "yang" that the state functions in a continual state of dynamic opposition between extremes. If, while exploring California, you find yourself in doubt about which half of the state you're in, here are a few telltale signs:

Southern California has palm trees; Northern California, redwoods.

Southern California has swimming pools; Northern California, hot tubs.

Southern California leads the world in missile production; Northern California makes computer chips instead.

Besides Anglos, the largest minority group in Southern California is Mexican; in Northern California, it's Chinese.

Southern California traces its origins to the birth of the motion picture industry; Northern California got its start half a century earlier with the Gold Rush.

Southern California is the nation's leading producer of citrus fruits; Northern California is the nation's number one producer of marijuana.

Southern California, the source of most television shows, shapes trends in mainstream America; Northern California, home of America's largest counterculture and gay communities, prides itself on being far out of the mainstream.

Southern California's elected representatives, including former U.S. Presidents Richard M. Nixon and Ronald Reagan and Governor (formerly San Diego Mayor and U.S. Senator) Pete Wilson, tend to be conservative Republicans; Northern California politicians, such as U.S. Senators Dianne Feinstein and Barbara Boxer, and former governor and presidential also-ran Edmund G. Brown, Jr., tend to be progressive Democrats.

When it comes to federal lands, Southern California has most of the state's Army, Navy, Marine, and Air Force bases and weapons testing ranges; Northern California has 90 percent of the national forests.

Seventy-five percent of the state's water comes from Northern California; 75 percent of it is consumed in the Southland, where billions of gallons are used to keep lawns alive in the desert while more environmentally minded Northern Californians conserve water by not flushing their toilets.

In short, Northern Californians see Southern California as a land of shopping malls, clogged freeways, violent crime, mind-numbing suburbia, and environmental irresponsibility. Southlanders see their northern neighbors as idealistic and perhaps dangerously fanatical New Age tree-huggers who should have stayed in the closet and wouldn't know the good life if they stepped in it. This perfect balance of opposites, more than any other factor, gives California its unique character.

Universal Studios Hollywood

Nothing captures Southern California's character and culture more than the entertainment industry

Unique Towns: Southern California

Ojai (pop. 7,600), surrounded by mountain peaks in a crescent valley north of Ventura, was selected by moviemakers as the exterior location for Shangri-La, the legendary utopia of the novel and classic film *Lost Horizon.* Its spectacular setting and its hot springs have made Ojai a mecca for tourists, artists, and alternative medicine practitioners ever since the first spa was opened there in 1870. The headquarters for several New Age sects, Ojai discourages newcomers with zoning and building regulations that are said to be the most restrictive on the west coast.

Pismo Beach (pop. 7,700) was a playground for movie stars in the 1930s and '40s, but its trendiness faded quickly. In later years, Pismo was best known for a species of large clam that was found only there, but too many clamdiggers eventually depleted the clam beds until restrictions had to be imposed on clamming. Today, this timeworn little town is known mainly for its sand dunes, the largest along Highway 1. Monarch butterflies migrate from Canada by the hundreds of thousands to doze the winter away on the branches of the "butterfly trees" of Pismo Beach.

Pismo Beach Chamber of Commerce

Even without its clams, Pismo Beach is worth a visit for its beautiful sand dunes and winter "butterfly trees"

Val Verde (pop. 1,100) is a forgotten old-time tourist getaway of a different kind. Founded in 1924 as an exclusively black resort at a time when segregation kept African American vacationers out of white resorts, the town developed into a community of elegant homes owned by the black elite of Los Angeles and was nicknamed "the Negro Palm Springs." Ironically, integration in the 1960s sent the town's tourist economy into decline. Today, it is a multicultural suburb of Los Angeles.

Solvang (pop. 4,700) was founded in 1911 by the Danish-American Corporation, an organization of midwestern professors of Danish descent. They established a school here to teach the Danish language, culture, and folkways. The school grew into a

Solvang is a Danish village transplanted to California's central valley

four-year liberal arts college but later closed down. Hans Christian Andersen would feel right at home in this fairy tale town, which is patterned after a traditional Danish village complete with windmills, gaslights, cobblestone sidewalks, and horse-drawn trolley.

Idyllwild (pop. 3,000), situated a mile high in the San Bernardino Mountains, is a little resort town surrounded by cool pine woodlands and rocky crags. The site of the prestigious Idyllwild School of Music and the Arts, the town also caters to backpackers and fishermen. This quiet mountain oasis makes a startling contrast to sun-drenched Palm Springs at the foot of the mountain.

Ten miles north of Barstow, the abandoned town of **Calico** is probably the best-known ghost town in the Mojave Desert. Restored as a San Bernardino Regional Park, it charges admission and offers narrow-gauge train rides and staged shootouts in the streets. A more authentic counterpart is the "living ghost town" of **Randsburg** (pop. 200), a former gold and silver camp that has never been entirely abandoned.

At the summit of Tejon Pass in the Tehachapi Mountains south of Bakersfield, **Lebec** (pop. 400) is a tiny tourist town with a single claim to fame: it was the headquarters of the United States Camel Corps. From 1854 to 1864, the Army used the beasts to carry supplies from San Antonio, Texas, through the heart of Apache country. The idea of California Camels is so strange that people around here haven't stopped talking about it yet. Living-history presentations and Civil War battle reenactments are held on a regular basis at the restored fort in town.

Unique Towns: Northern California

Residents of **Boonville** (pop. 750), an out-of-the way ranching town in Mendocino County, invented their own language, called Boontling, in the 1880s and spoke it almost exclusively through the 1920s. Many of their descendents still speak Boontling as a second language. Curious travelers go miles out of the way in hopes of eavesdropping on a conversation between locals.

Ferndale (pop. 1,350), south of Eureka on the back road to the Lost Coast, calls itself a "Victorian Village" because of its meticulously preserved 1880s architecture. The gingerbread trim has been repainted in new, chic color schemes, and buildings that were once feed stores and saloons now house cute tourist shops; as a blemish-free evocation of a bygone era, Ferndale compares favorably to Disneyland's Main Street.

Bob von Normann/FVN Corp.

Ferndale's architecture recalls a bygone era

The company town of **Scotia** (pop. 850), south of Eureka on scenic Highway 101, has been owned and operated by the Pacific Lumber Company since 1869. The company provides housing, schools, health care, and even churches for workers at the largest lumber mill in the United States, which slices up 2,000-year-old redwoods. Scotia was seen by many as a utopian community until 1986, when Pacific Lumber was taken over by multinational investors whose plans to greatly increase redwood cutting sparked environmentalist protests.

Bodie (pop. 0) stands as a showpiece among the many ghost towns left over from the late 19th-century gold rush in the Mammoth Lakes area. The abandoned town, which once had a population of more than 10,000, was taken over by the government in 1964 to become a State Historic Park. Interpretive signs tell visitors all about the town and mines, providing insights for those who may want to explore other abandoned towns in the area, such as nearby Rattlesnake Gulch.

Trinidad (pop. 400) may have the most idyllic setting on the entire California coast. The town sits on a rocky headland above one of California's oldest fishing marinas. A 3-mile scenic drive from town takes visitors to picture-perfect little beaches bounded by redwood groves. There's even a small, romantic lighthouse.

Big Sur (pop. 1,500), on the coast 25 miles south of Carmel, is a community trying hard not to be a town at all. Lacking a town center, expensive homes and country stores straggle along 6 miles of the Big Sur River amid towering mountains, ocean lookouts, lush canyons, and the southernmost coastal redwood groves. Author Henry Miller made his home there for 18 years and was eventually joined by other counterculture figures, including Jack Kerouac, Richard Brautigan, and Joan Baez. The area is also known as the site of the Esalen Institute, a premier center for consciousness-raising symposiums.

Point Arena (pop. 400), on Highway 1 in Mendocino County, is a small fishing village as unspoiled as any along the California coast. Its lighthouse, a favorite spot for whalewatching, replaced an earlier lighthouse destroyed by the San Francisco earthquake of 1906—even though it's 130 miles from San Francisco. Point Arena is situated precisely on the northern end of the San Andreas Fault.

The Pacific Lumber Company

Scotia, a lumber company town since 1869

Offbeat Festivals and Holidays

Every California town, it seems, has at least one annual special event designed both to rouse local spirit and to attract tourists. The competition has grown so tough that many towns have resorted to increasingly spectacular displays to attract attention. Here are a few worth checking out:

San Francisco Convention & Visitors Bureau

Chinatown's Grant Avenue becomes an outdoor stage during San Francisco's Chinese New Year Festival

January: Believe it or not, sunny Palm Springs sponsors annual **Sled Dog Races** in the nearby mountains.

February: The **Chinese New Year** is celebrated with fireworks and costumed parades in both Los Angeles and San Francisco. Camel races are the main event at the **National Date Festival** in Indio. The competitive spirit also takes hold up north in Crescent City, home of the **World Championship Crab Races**.

March: The public can't get tickets to attend the **Academy Awards** in downtown Los Angeles, but the Academy of Motion Picture Arts and Sciences thoughtfully provides bleachers outside for stargazers with binoculars. Another of the state's premier social events is the **California Wine Festival** in Monterey. Mendocino offers not only wine tasting but also cruises and an art show during its annual **Whale Festival.**

April: In San Francisco's Japantown, the **Cherry Blossom Festival** is unsurpassed in its pageantry and spectacle.

May: **Cinco de Mayo**, the Mexican holiday celebrating the overthrow of the Emperor Maximillian by Benito Juárez, occasions street celebrations in Los Angeles on Olvera Street and elsewhere, as well as in San Jose. In Angels Camp, the annual **Jumping Frog Jubilee** re-creates the contest immortalized in Mark Twain's short story. Coulterville sponsors its annual **Coyote Howling Contest.**

June: Elaborate and outrageous costumes add pizzazz to the already colorful gay and lesbian parades held in both San Francisco and Los Angeles on **Gay Freedom Day**.

July: The **Festival of Arts and Pageant of the Masters** in Laguna Beach features actors in living tableaux re-creating classic paintings on stage. A garlic-eating contest is the climax for Gilroy's annual **Garlic Festival** (no vampires, please). Meanwhile, Smith River holds its **Easter in July Lily Festival.**

August: Santa Barbara's **Old Spanish Days Fiesta** is the most elaborate of all the festivals honoring the state's early Hispanic heritage. The **Renaissance Pleasure Faire** in Novato, north of San Francisco, is the oldest and largest fair of its kind. The **California State Fair** is held in Sacramento.

September: The **Valley of the Moon Vintage Festival** in Sonoma is one of the Wine Country's top tasting events. Festivities surround the **Poison Oak Show** in Columbia.

October: **Columbus Day**, the biggest festival day of the year in San Francisco's North Beach, features a parade, the blessing of the fishing fleet, and a reenactment of Columbus' landing. Half Moon Bay holds its annual **Art and Pumpkin Festival**, including a pumpkin parade, a week before Hallowe'en.

November: Pasadena holds its huge, wild, and crazy **Doo Dah Parade** for residents with float ideas too bizarre for the city's famous Rose Bowl Parade in January. Not to be outdone, El Cajon holds its annual **Mother Goose Parade**. Arts, crafts, and live music are the order of the day at Mendocino's lively **Thanksgiving Festival.**

December: Newport Beach's dazzling **Christmas Boat Parade** repeats for six nights before Christmas. The traditional Mexican **Las Posadas** Christmas Pageant is held in several Southern California communities, including San Diego, Los Angeles, and San Luis Obispo.

San Francisco Convention & Visitors Bureau

The sake barrel shrine provides the finale for San Francisco's Cherry Blossom Festival, held every April

KIDS' ADVENTURES

Amusement and Theme Parks

Knott's Berry Farm

Knott's Berry Farm has great roller coasters

The most famous kids' place in California is **Disneyland**, right? Lots of parents like to take their families there because they remember their own childhood visits to Disneyland. It's as great now as it was then—probably even better, because of big new rides like Splash Mountain and Space Mountain. ***FYI:*** 1313 Harbor Blvd., Anaheim; 714-999-4565.

Let's say you've done everything there is to do at Disneyland and it's not time to go home yet. Southern California has lots of amusement parks. One that has been famous for fifty years is **Knotts Berry Farm**. This place grows huge fields of boysenberries for jams and jellies, but your reason for visiting it is the roller coasters—a corkscrew roller coaster and another, bigger one called Montezooma's Revenge. ***FYI:*** 8039 Beach Boulevard, Buena Park; 714-827-1776.

And if that's not enough, try **Six Flags Magic Mountain**'s more than 100 rides, including a roller coaster that does a really scary double loop. There are also two other roller coasters—one called Colossus because it is so big and a diving coaster called Flashback. ***FYI:*** Magic Mountain Parkway, Valencia; 818-992-0884.

Museums Especially for Kids

You've seen science museums for kids before, but San Francisco's **Exploratorium** is really different. Artists helped design this hands-on museum, and it's more fun than being inside a video game. Many of the 500 exhibits in this huge warehouse space deal with the human senses. There are computers, laser beams, and a Tactile Dome you explore by feeling around in the dark. Instead of guards like most museums have, orange-suited Explainers help you figure out how the exhibits work. ***FYI:*** In the Palace of Fine Arts, Marina Boulevard at Lyon Street; 415-561-4115.

The **Los Angeles Children's Museum** offers different kinds of thrills, giving kids a chance to do many things they are not allowed to do elsewhere. You can ride a police motorcycle, ambulance, or street sweeper, paint your face, or dress up like a fireman. There is a big playroom called "Sticky City" full of Velcro-covered cushions that you can build into whatever you want. ***FYI:*** 310 North Main Street; 213-687-8801.

Exploratorium

Kids love the huge bubble hoop at San Francisco's Exploratorium

The Fanciest Ship and the Biggest Airplane

In Long Beach, you can board the ocean liner ***Queen Mary***, the most elegant ship to sail the seas in the 1930s. Back then, there were no jetliners to fly people between Europe and the U.S., so people crossed the ocean in ships like this one. It took about two weeks. A tour of the *Queen Mary* even takes you deep into the ship's holds to see the huge engines that drove it. ***FYI:*** Pier J, Long Beach; 310-435-3511.

Under the dome right next to the *Queen Mary* is the ***Spruce Goose***, the biggest wooden airplane ever built. Howard Hughes designed it to carry soldiers in World War II. The trouble was, it did not fly very well. After the plane was tested once, it never flew again.

Cowboy Museums

The **Gene Autry Western Heritage Museum** in Griffith Park recalls the days when most Hollywood movies were about cowboys. There are horses, saddles, guns, fancy outfits worn by old-time cowboy stars like Gene Autry and Hopalong Cassidy, and short films about how western movies were made. ***FYI:*** 4700 Western Heritage Way; 213-667-2000.

Another long-time cowboy hero is remembered at the **Roy Rogers-Dale Evans Museum,** 15650 Seneca Road, Victorville; 619-243-4547.

Animal Parks

Everybody says the **San Diego Zoo** in Balboa Park is the best in the world, and they're right. This zoo has more than 3,500 animals and birds—500 species in all. Part of what makes it so special is the Skyfari, an aerial tram 170 feet above the zoo. You can also walk through a 3-acre rain forest and on the boardwalk that zigzags through the huge aviary with thousands of free-flying birds. Instead of cages, animal habitats are surrounded by moats and are big enough so the tigers and bears seem to be loose. Koalas and hummingbirds have special habitats. *FYI:* 619-234-3153.

San Diego Animal Park, not in San Diego but 30 miles outside the city, in Escondido, is owned and operated by the zoo. In many ways, the animal park is better than the zoo—a huge open area of 2,100 acres that resembles the African veldt. The animals roam free, while you watch them from a train on the 5-mile-long monorail track. You can also walk up and down hill after hill on the Kilimanjaro Hiking Trail. It does not go where the animals are, though it may feel like they are all around you. The trail actually takes you to a series of overlooks where you can see giraffes and zebras grazing on the veldt. It is kind of like Jurassic Park, except that instead of tyrannosauruses there are rhinoceroses—an endangered species, but not nearly as endangered as you would be if you got too close. *FYI:* 619-480-0100.

Susan Kaye/San Diego Conv. & Visitors Bureau

Animals roam free at the San Diego Animal Park

There are also the **Los Angeles Zoo** (5333 Zoo Drive; 213-666-4090) in Griffith Park with 2,000 animals, and the **San Francisco Zoo** (Sloat Boulevard at 45th Avenue; 415-753-7083) with 1,000 animals.

Several other California towns have smaller zoos, such as Merced, San Rafael, Fresno, Atascadero, Oakland, Folsom, San Jose, Sacramento, Santa Ana, Santa Barbara, Eureka, and Sonoma.

The **California Center for Wildlife** in San Rafael, north of San Francisco, is for injured wild animals and big birds like hawks and owls. Caretakers help them heal and return to the wild. *FYI:* 76 Albert Park Lane; 415-456-7283.

Marine World/Africa USA

A young visitor gets a kiss from a California sea lion at Marine World/Africa USA

The **Exotic Feline Breeding Compound** in Rosamond is part of a captive breeding program to save such endangered species as tigers, jaguars, mountain lions, leopards, and ocelots. There are about forty big cats in the compound, and you can see them all on a guided tour. ***FYI:*** Rhyolite Road; 805-256-3332.

In San Diego, **Sea World** (Sea World Drive; 619-226-3901) shows feature orcas trained to do tricks, like in *Free Willy.* You might feel sorry for the whales and dolphins, but the Forbidden Reef, teeming with stingrays and moray eels, is worth seeing. There is an even bigger trained whale and dolphin show at **Marine World Africa USA** (Marine World Parkway; 707-643-6722) in the Bay Area city of Vallejo. Here you'll see not only dolphins and sea lions but also trained chimpanzees, elephants, and tigers.

But if you really want to learn about sea creatures, the place to go is an aquarium. The best one in California, probably in the whole U.S., is the **Monterey Bay Aquarium** (886 Cannery Row; 408-648-4888). It has a two-story sea-otter exhibit, an underwater kelp forest, an aviary of shore birds, and a "touch pool" where you can hold starfish and other strange tide pool creatures. Southern California's best aquarium is **Scripps Aquarium-Museum** (8602 La Jolla Shores Drive, La Jolla; 619-534-6933), part of the Scripps Institute of Oceanography, where scientists from all over the world come to study the sea.

Tracking the Stars

Back in the old days, tour guides would drive people around in open-air buses to see the homes of famous movie stars. Today, big stars' houses are not so easy to find. There are still home tours of Beverly Hills, but they mostly show where old-time celebrities lived when movies were black-and-white.

Checking out the hand prints of the stars outside Mann's Chinese Theater in Hollywood

Los Angeles CVB/Michele & Tom Grimm

You probably won't see any movie stars in Hollywood, either, but you can check out the sidewalk in front of **Mann's Chinese Theater** (6925 Hollywood Boulevard; 213-464-8111) and see where more than 160 of the all-time most famous screen idols signed their names in wet cement and left their footprints, leg prints, ear prints, or other impressions for future generations to admire. The theater itself, a gaudy Hollywood version of a Chinese pagoda, is one of the last old-time "picture palaces" where thousands of people came to watch movies in the days before television. Right down the street is another landmark picture palace, the **Egyptian Theater** (6712 Hollywood Boulevard; 213-467-6167), built by Sid Graumann, who also built the Chinese Theater. It was inspired by the then-recent discovery of King Tut's tomb in Egypt. The two theaters often show "first cuts" to find out whether people like a movie before it is distributed all over the country. Watch for people with clipboards in front of the Chinese Theater; they give away free movie tickets.

If you want to see real movie stars, the place to start is the **Motion Picture Coordination Office** (622 Hollywood Boulevard, 213-485-5324). They give out "shoot sheets" that tell where around the city movies, TV shows, and music videos are being filmed. You can often watch them from a distance.

You can take different kinds of movie and TV studio tours around Los Angeles. The biggest, longest, and most exciting is

Universal Studios. It is so huge that it feels like a Disneyland theme park as the tram carries you through real-life re-creations of movie special effects. The tour features bombs, shoot-outs, fires, an 8.3 earthquake, King Kong, and E.T.—and it lasts six hours. ***FYI:*** 100 Universal City Plaza; 818-508-9600.

Los Angeles CVB/Michele & Tom Grimm

Touring the Warner Bros. back lot in beautiful downtown Burbank

If you really want to see how films are made (instead of how they are turned into theme park rides), the place to go is **Burbank Studios**, where Warner Brothers shoots movies and TV shows. The two-hour walking tour does not usually have any monsters or explosions, but it does take you inside the wardrobe department, set construction shop, sound stages, back lot sets, and animation studios. Visitors often get to see actors and directors at work. ***FYI:*** 4000 Warner Boulevard, Burbank; 818-954-1744. Reservations are necessary.

TV shows are a lot different from movies, as you will find out if you visit **NBC Studios**. You get to see what TV sets are like and how they do video special effects. People who take the 1¼-hour studio tour get to be in a simulated game show. If you go early in the day, you can usually get free tickets to be in the *Tonight Show* audience that evening. ***FYI:*** 3000 West Alameda Street, Burbank; 818-840-3537.

You can also get free tickets to TV shows from **CBS Ticket Information** (7800 Beverly Boulevard; 213-852-2624) and **Fox Television Center** (5746 Sunset Boulevard; 818-506-0067).

And for Dessert . . .

If you are in San Francisco, do whatever it takes to get your parents to drive you across the Bay Bridge to Oakland (or take you there on the BART train). That's where you will find **Fenton's Creamery**, and most people who go there think it is the best soda shop in the world. Fenton's makes its own ice cream from scratch and serves really huge hot chocolate and butterscotch sundaes and banana splits. I mean, we're talking *really* huge here—sometimes whole families can't finish one of their banana splits. Try one and you will remember it for a long time. ***FYI:*** 4226 Piedmont Avenue, Oakland; 510-658-7000.

On Fisherman's Wharf, the sign for **Blue Chip Cookies of San Francisco** says they are the "best cookies in the country." They are near the Guinness Book of World Records Museum and Ripley's Believe It or Not! Museum, and most people think they are extra good cookies. But not nearly as big as Fenton's ice cream concoctions.

A lot of other ice cream shops around Northern California try to imitate Fenton's. Even if they are not quite as good, you will be glad to find them when your family goes on a long drive somewhere that might not be too interesting for kids, like the Wine Country. The **Old Sonoma Creamery** has great homemade ice cream, and it is easier to get your parents to take you there because it also serves sandwiches and makes a good lunch stop. It is right on the town plaza. ***FYI:*** 400 1st Street East, Sonoma; 707-938-2938.

Mexican Desserts

If you go to Olvera Street in Los Angeles, you will find a lot of vendors selling Mexican food from carts. Some of them sell *flan*, a kind of caramel custard that is everybody's favorite dessert in Mexico. Be sure to try it and find out why.

Berkeley Historical Society

Lucy Wang with some of her Chinese desserts

Chinese Desserts

If you go to Chinatown, either in San Francisco or Los Angeles, you will see that Chinese Americans have other desserts besides fortune cookies, including some you might never have tasted before. One favorite is almond-flavored gelatin. It tastes like candy and wiggles like Jell-O.

Desert Desserts

A lot of tourist stores in the desert sell jars of honey or, better yet, honeycombs. Honeybees thrive in the desert. Beekeepers started hives around San Diego in 1853, when they brought thousands of bees from Italy. Today, more honey comes from Southern California than from the rest of the U.S. put together—about 12,000 tons a year. Most of the bee ranches, called apiaries, are around Bakersfield. It's a good business, because the beekeepers don't just make money by selling the honey. They also charge local fruit and nut farmers for the bees' pollinating services.

Honey isn't the only thing in the desert good for a sweet tooth. **Julian**, an Old West-style town at the edge of Anza-Borrego Desert State Park, is one of the few places in California where they grow apples. In nearby Santa Ysabel, **Dudley's Bakery** is famous for its apple pies. Some people drive all the way from L.A. to buy pies there. ***FYI:*** 800-225-3348.

INDEX

Other Books from John Muir Publications

Travel Books by Rick Steves
Asia Through the Back Door, 4th ed., 400 pp. $16.95
Europe 101: History and Art for the Traveler, 4th ed., 372 pp. $15.95
Europe Through the Back Door, 12th ed., 434 pp. $17.95
Europe Through the Back Door Phrase Book: French, 112 pp. $4.95
Europe Through the Back Door Phrase Book: German, 112 pp. $4.95
Europe Through the Back Door Phrase Book: Italian, 112 pp. $4.95
Europe Through the Back Door Phrase Book: Spanish & Portuguese, 288 pp. $6.95
Mona Winks: Self-Guided Tours of Europe's Top Museums, 2nd ed., 456 pp. $16.95
See the 2 to 22 Days series to follow for other Rick Steves titles.

A Natural Destination Series
Belize: A Natural Destination, 2nd ed., 304 pp. $16.95
Costa Rica: A Natural Destination, 3rd ed., 400 pp. $17.95
Guatemala: A Natural Destination, 336 pp. $16.95

Undiscovered Islands Series
Undiscovered Islands of the Caribbean, 3rd ed., 264 pp. $14.95
Undiscovered Islands of the Mediterranean, 2nd ed., 256 pp. $13.95
Undiscovered Islands of the U.S. and Canadian West Coast, 288 pp. $12.95

For Birding Enthusiasts
The Birder's Guide to Bed and Breakfasts, U.S. and Canada, 288 pp. $15.95
The Visitor's Guide to the Birds of the Central National Parks: U.S. and Canada, 400 pp. $15.95
The Visitor's Guide to the Birds of the Eastern National Parks: U.S. and Canada, 400 pp. $15.95
The Visitor's Guide to the Birds of the Rocky Mountain National Parks, U.S. and Canada, 432 pp. $15.95

Unique Travel Series
Each is 112 pages and $10.95 paper.
Unique Arizona
Unique California
Unique Colorado
Unique Florida
Unique New England
Unique New Mexico
Unique Texas
Unique Washington (available 11/94)

2 to 22 Days Series
Each title offers 22 flexible daily itineraries useful for planning vacations of any length. Included are "must see" attractions as well as hidden "jewels."
2 to 22 Days in the American Southwest, 1994 ed., 192 pp. $10.95
2 to 22 Days in Asia, 1994 ed., 176 pp. $10.95
2 to 22 Days in Australia, 1994 ed., 192 pp. $10.95
2 to 22 Days in California, 1994 ed., 192 pp. $10.95
2 to 22 Days in Eastern Canada, 1994 ed., 192 pp. $12.95
2 to 22 Days in Europe, 1994 ed., 304 pp. $14.95
2 to 22 Days in Florida, 1994 ed., 192 pp. $10.95
2 to 22 Days in France, 1994 ed., 192 pp. $10.95
2 to 22 Days in Germany, Austria, and Switzerland, 1994 ed., 240 pp. $12.95
2 to 22 Days in Great Britain, 1994 ed., 208 pp. $10.95
2 to 22 Days Around the Great Lakes, 1994 ed., 192 pp. $10.95
2 to 22 Days in Hawaii, 1994 ed., 192 pp. $10.95
2 to 22 Days in Italy, 1994 ed., 208 pp. $10.95
2 to 22 Days in New England, 1994 ed., 192 pp. $10.95
2 to 22 Days in New Zealand, 1994 ed., 192 pp. $10.95
2 to 22 Days in Norway, Sweden, and Denmark, 1994 ed., 192 pp. $10.95
2 to 22 Days in the Pacific Northwest, 1994 ed., 192 pp. $10.95
2 to 22 Days in the Rockies, 1994 ed., 192 pp. $10.95
2 to 22 Days in Spain and Portugal, 1994 ed., 208 pp. $10.95
2 to 22 Days in Texas, 1994 ed., 192 pp. $10.95
2 to 22 Days in Thailand, 1994 ed., 192 pp. $10.95
22 Days (or More) Around the World, 1994 ed., 264 pp. $13.95

Other Terrific Travel Titles
The 100 Best Small Art Towns in America, 224 pp. $12.95
Elderhostels: The Students' Choice, 2nd ed., 304 pp. $15.95
Environmental Vacations: Volunteer Projects to Save the Planet, 2nd ed., 248 pp. $16.95
A Foreign Visitor's Guide to America, 224 pp. $12.95
Great Cities of Eastern Europe, 256 pp. $16.95
Indian America: A Traveler's Companion, 3rd ed., 432 pp. $18.95
Interior Furnishings Southwest, 256 pp. $19.95
Opera! The Guide to Western Europe's Great Houses, 296 pp. $18.95
Paintbrushes and Pistols: How the Taos Artists Sold the West, 288 pp. $17.95
The People's Guide to Mexico, 9th ed., 608 pp. $18.95
Ranch Vacations: The Complete Guide to Guest and Resort, Fly-Fishing, and Cross-Country Skiing Ranches, 3rd ed., 512 pp. $19.95
The Shopper's Guide to Art and Crafts in the Hawaiian Islands, 272 pp. $13.95
The Shopper's Guide to Mexico, 224 pp. $9.95
Understanding Europeans, 272 pp. $14.95
A Viewer's Guide to Art: A Glossary of Gods, People, and Creatures, 144 pp. $10.95
Watch It Made in the U.S.A.: A Visitor's Guide to the Companies that Make Your Favorite Products, 272 pp. $16.95

Parenting Titles
Being a Father: Family, Work, and Self, 176 pp. $12.95
Preconception: A Woman's Guide to Preparing for Pregnancy and Parenthood, 232 pp. $14.95
Schooling at Home: Parents, Kids, and Learning, 264 pp., $14.95
Teens: A Fresh Look, 240 pp. $14.95

Automotive Titles
The Greaseless Guide to Car Care Confidence, 224 pp. $14.95
How to Keep Your Datsun/Nissan Alive, 544 pp. $21.95
How to Keep Your Subaru Alive, 480 pp. $21.95
How to Keep Your Toyota Pickup Alive, 392 pp. $21.95
How to Keep Your VW Alive, 25thAnniversary ed., 464 pp. spiral bound $25

TITLES FOR YOUNG READERS AGES 8 AND UP

American Origins Series
Each is 48 pages and $12.95 hardcover.
Tracing Our English Roots (available 1/95)
Tracing Our French Roots (available 1/95)
Tracing Our German Roots
Tracing Our Irish Roots
Tracing Our Italian Roots
Tracing Our Japanese Roots (available 12/94)
Tracing Our Jewish Roots
Tracing Our Polish Roots

Bizarre & Beautiful Series
Each is 48 pages, $9.95 paper, and $14.95 hardcover.
Bizarre & Beautiful Ears
Bizarre & Beautiful Eyes
Bizarre & Beautiful Feelers
Bizarre & Beautiful Noses
Bizarre & Beautiful Tongues

Environmental Titles
Habitats: Where the Wild Things Live, 48 pp. $9.95
The Indian Way: Learning to Communicate with Mother Earth, 114 pp. $9.95
Rads, Ergs, and Cheeseburgers: The Kids' Guide to Energy and the Environment, 108 pp. $13.95
The Kids' Environment Book: What's Awry and Why, 192 pp. $13.95

Extremely Weird Series
Each is 48 pages, $9.95 paper, and $14.95 hardcover.
Extremely Weird Bats
Extremely Weird Birds
Extremely Weird Endangered Species
Extremely Weird Fishes
Extremely Weird Frogs
Extremely Weird Insects
Extremely Weird Mammals
Extremely Weird Micro Monsters
Extremely Weird Primates
Extremely Weird Reptiles
Extremely Weird Sea Creatures
Extremely Weird Snakes
Extremely Weird Spiders

Kidding Around Travel Series
All are 64 pages and $9.95 paper, except for *Kidding Around Spain* and *Kidding Around the National Parks of the Southwest*, which are 108 pages and $12.95 paper.
Kidding Around Atlanta
Kidding Around Boston, 2nd ed.
Kidding Around Chicago, 2nd ed.
Kidding Around the Hawaiian Islands
Kidding Around London
Kidding Around Los Angeles
Kidding Around the National Parks of the Southwest
Kidding Around New York City, 2nd ed.
Kidding Around Paris
Kidding Around Philadelphia
Kidding Around San Diego
Kidding Around San Francisco
Kidding Around Santa Fe
Kidding Around Seattle
Kidding Around Spain
Kidding Around Washington, D.C., 2nd ed.

Kids Explore Series
Written by kids for kids, all are $9.95 paper.
Kids Explore America's African American Heritage, 128 pp.
Kids Explore the Gifts of Children with Special Needs, 128 pp.
Kids Explore America's Hispanic Heritage, 112 pp.
Kids Explore America's Japanese American Heritage, 144 pp.

Masters of Motion Series
Each is 48 pages and $9.95 paper.
How to Drive an Indy Race Car
How to Fly a 747
How to Fly the Space Shuttle

Rainbow Warrior Artists Series
Each is 48 pages and $14.95 hardcover.
Native Artists of Africa
Native Artists of Europe
Native Artists of North America

Rough and Ready Series
Each is 48 pages and $12.95 hardcover.
Rough and Ready Cowboys
Rough and Ready Homesteaders
Rough and Ready Loggers
Rough and Ready Outlaws and Lawmen
Rough and Ready Prospectors
Rough and Ready Railroaders

X-ray Vision Series
Each is 48 pages and $9.95 paper.
Looking Inside the Brain
Looking Inside Cartoon Animation
Looking Inside Caves and Caverns
Looking Inside Sports Aerodynamics
Looking Inside Sunken Treasures
Looking Inside Telescopes and the Night Sky

Ordering Information
Please check your local bookstore, or call **1-800-888-7504** to order direct. All orders are shipped via UPS; see chart below to calculate charges for U.S. destinations. **No post office boxes please; we must have a street address to ensure delivery**. If the book you request is not available, we will hold your check until we can ship it. Foreign orders are shipped surface rate unless otherwise requested; enclose $3 for the first item and $1 for each additional item.

For U.S. Orders Totaling	Add
Up to $15.00	$4.25
$15.01 to $45.00	$5.25
$45.01 to $75.00	$6.25
$75.01 or more	$7.25

Methods of Payment
Check, money order, American Express, MasterCard, or Visa. We cannot be responsible for cash sent through the mail. For credit card orders, include your card number, expiration date, and your signature, or call **1-800-888-7504**. American Express card orders can only be shipped to billing address of cardholder. Sorry, no C.O.D.'s. Residents of sunny New Mexico, add 6.25% tax to total.

Address all orders and inquiries to:
John Muir Publications
P.O. Box 613
Santa Fe, NM 87504
(505) 982-4078
(800) 888-7504